Bury F.C.
FA Cup Scrapbook 1900 & 1903

Shakin `em up for t`Cup

Published by Don Gillan - MMXVIII
Copyright © Don Gillan, September 2018 – All rights reserved.

Manuscript created entirely in Libre Office
the World's best FREE office productivity suite.
https://www.libreoffice.org/

Van Houten's Cocoa

"OFF TO SCHOOL."

Whether at home or at school, sustaining and invigorating food is a necessity for growing boys and girls, and there is no food beverage equal to Van Houten's Cocoa for building up and invigorating the system. Parents cannot always regulate the children's diet while at school, but they can make

van Houten's Cocoa

the beverage of the home and so ensure that young and old alike may enjoy a beverage

unequalled for

DELICIOUS NATURAL FLAVOR.
NOURISHING & INVIGORATING PROPERTIES.

BEST & GOES FARTHEST.

FOREWORD

Bury F.C. surprised the football world when the club from the relatively minor Lancashire town not only won promotion to the First League but then went on to establish themselves as equals amongst such larger town and city clubs as the Blackburn Rovers, Everton, Preston North End and Aston Villa. By the turn of the century the club were in their fifth consecutive season among the elite and headed for their first F.A. Cup Final. Not only did they win the trophy at the end of that season, they repeated their triumph again just three years later. At that time they were able to make the proud boast of having won ten out of twelve Cup finals they had contested in their brief history, i.e: English Cup, winners 1900, 1903; Lancashire Senior Cup, Winners 1892, 1899, 1903; and Manchester Cup Winners 1894, 1896, 1897, 1900, 1903 (beaten finalists 1895, 1899). The greatest honours, of course, were those two English F.A. Cup wins, and this is the story of those two successes, as told through the press of the time. All matches of both finalists in both seasons covered, including full period match report, with additional facts and commentary by the author.

Previous Publications in the "Scrapbook" series of vintage football histories:

Bradford City Season Scrapbook 1902/03-03/04: Changing Codes.
Bradford City Season Scrapbook 1907/08: Second Division Champions.
Bradford Park Avenue Season Scrapbook 1907/08: A Southern Adventure
Everton Season Scrapbook 1890/91: Anfield Champions in Blue
Leeds United Season Scrapbook 1919/20-20/21: From The Ashes.
Preston North End Season Scrapbook 1888/89: The Invincibles
Sunderland/Sunderland Albion Season Scrapbook 1891/92: The Mighty and the Fallen
The Wednesday Season Scrapbook 1889/90: Days of Alliance
Liverpool Season Scrapbook 1892/93 & 94/94: Before They Were Red
Bradford City F.A. Cup Scrapbook 1911: How t'Cup Came Home to Bradford
Sheffield United F.A. Cup Scrapbook 1899-1902: The Three Cups
Tottenham Hotspur F.A. Cup Scrapbook 1901: 'Spurs First Cup

Rev. 1.01

SOME NOTES ON FOOTBALL IN 1900-1903

There were some significant differences in the way the Association game was played and organised during the period to which this publication relates, as compared to the current day. To enable readers to better understand the period match reports reproduced in this publication, let me first summarise the more significant of these differences, particularly with reference to any terms which may be used in these reports that are not so common in the current day.

Formation – The predominant playing formation of the era was 2-3-5, ie:
Outside Left – Inside Left – Centre Forward – Inside Right – Outside Right
(forwards)
Left Half – Centre Half - Right Half
(halves)
Left Back – Right Back
(backs)
Goalkeeper

Substitutes – match teams consisted of eleven players only, with **no** substitutes. Substitutes were not permitted in English League Football until the 1965-66 season. Prior to then, if a player was unable for any reason to continue to fully participate in the game then his team would have to play on a man short, or, in the case of the 'walking wounded', with the injured player switched to a less critical position - usually an outside wing where he would not compromise his teams defence and might still contribute to the attack with the occasional pass if the ball happened his way.

Players Kit – Players shirts bore neither numbers nor names for identification.

Goalkeepers - Goalkeepers wore exactly the same strip as the outfield players of the same team (although woollen jerseys of the same colour might be substituted for cotton shirts). The rule requiring goalkeepers to wear distinctive tops (so they could be distinguished by referees in a melee of players) was not introduced until 1909. Goalkeepers could take no more than two steps with the ball in their hands before releasing it. Bouncing the ball off the ground reset the count. The number of steps permitted was later extended to four and subsequently replaced by the loosely enforced 'six second' rule.

Off-side – A player was off-side if there were less than **three** opponents between him and the opposing goal line at the moment when the ball was played forward to him by a member of his own side. The goalkeeper counted as, but needed not necessarily to be, one of the three. The required number of opponents was reduced to two from 1925. A player in an off-side position could be "played on" if an opponent made any contact with the ball (including accidental) before it reached him.

Floodlights – Although Floodlighting in association football dates as far back as 1878, when experimental floodlit matches were played at Bramall Lane, they did not become a regular part of the game until the 1950's. All competitive matches had to be timed so as to complete in daylight hours.

Match Ball – Match balls were made of stitched leather panels and were much heavier than modern footballs made of lightweight synthetic materials. Furthermore, in wet conditions a ball could more than double in weight due to the leather skin becoming waterlogged.

Divisions – The League was divided into only two divisions – First and Second. It was not until the 1920's that the League expanded – by adding two initially regional third divisions which later became nationalised as Divisions Three and Four.

Re-Election – The three clubs finishing in the last three places in the Second Division were automatically stripped of their League status. In order to continue playing League Football they would then have to apply for re-election, and their application, along with those of any would-be newcomers, would be voted upon by the remaining clubs.

Charging (a.k.a. Shoulder Charge) – A form of tackle wherein the tackler makes deliberate bodily contact with an opponent, leading with his shoulder against the opponents shoulder, in an effort to barge the opponent off the ball. This was/is legitimate so long as each player had/has one foot on the ground at the time of contact, and the amount of force used was/is not 'excessive'. Charging remains in the rules today, but the idea of what is regarded as excessive is now applied so stringently that the forceful charging of old has gone from the game.

£ s. d. - U.K. Pre-decimalisation currency: pounds (£ - librae), shillings (s - solidi) and pence (d - denarii) where 1s = 12d : £1 = 20s (or 240d). Allowing for inflation, the sum of £1 in 1900 would be worth approximately the equivalent of £123 at 2018 prices[1].

Linesmen – the common term for referees assistants in the days before political correctness.

Goal Average – Used in league tables to rank teams on equal points. Was more precise (therefore less prone to produce equal results), but less easy to calculate than Goal Difference (as used today). Calculated by dividing goals for by goals against - the higher the result the better.

Official Scorers – In the match reports reproduced in this book the scorers indicated may occasionally differ from those indicated in the official records. This is understandable at a time when players did not wear numbers to aid identification.

Pitch Markings – Football is continually evolving, with new innovations and small rule changes occurring on a regular basis. This was especially true during the first fifty years following the inception of the F.A., during which time the game changed substantially: e.g. two unconnected upright posts were replaced by a frame to which a net was later added; one of the eleven players became a goalkeeper with the privilege

---

1 Source: http://inflation.stephenmorley.org.

of handling the ball; and pitch markings evolved from none at all (just four flags signifying the corners) to almost their modern standard. In regard to the latter, even in the four year span covered by this book pitch markings altered substantially. The markings introduced in 1902 are the same as in use today (2018) apart from the absence of the 'D' on the penalty box – which was added later.

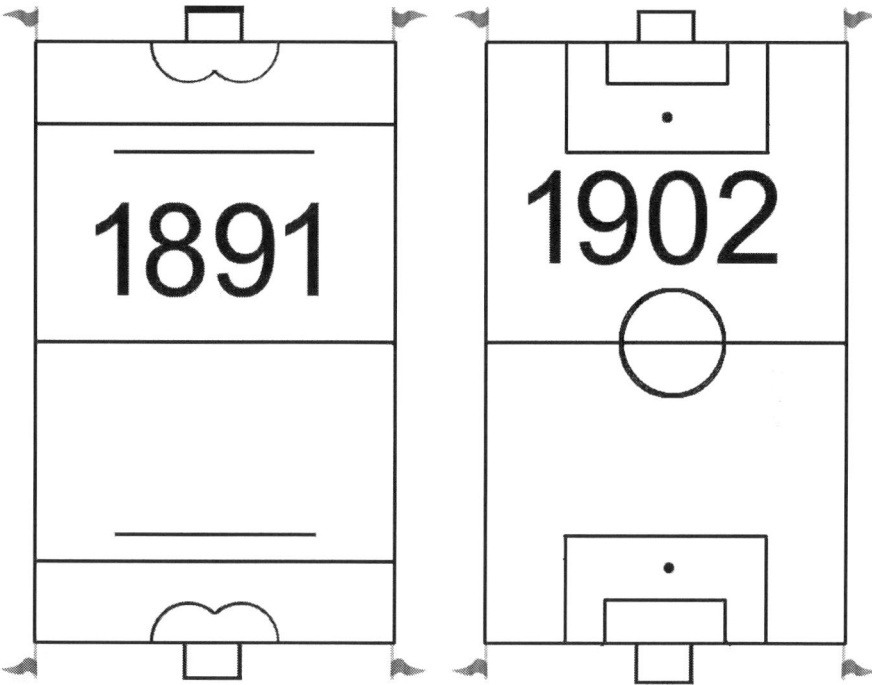

In the 1891 standard the solid line the width of the pitch is the penalty line – penalties could be awarded for infringements occurring behind this line and the kick taken from any point along the line. The incomplete line indicates the distance other players must retire whilst the kick is taken.

The F.A. Challenge Cup

The current F.A. Challenge Cup trophy is actually the second of it's kind by design and the fifth by manufacture.

1. The first cup was used from 1872 to 1895 (stolen).
2. A duplicate copy of the first cup was manufactured and used from 1896 to 1910 (retired due to existence of unauthorised duplicate).
3. A new copyrighted design was introduced in 1911 and used until 1991 (retired due to wear and tear having caused the trophy to become fragile).
4. An exact duplicate was introduced in 1992 and used until 2013 (retired due to wear and tear).
5. Another but more sturdily constructed duplicate was introduced in 2014.

The origins of the F.A. Cup can be traced back to a meeting of the Football Association on July 20th, 1871, where it was proposed by C.W. Alcock, Secretary of the F.A., that a Challenge Cup be instituted for which all clubs belonging to the Association should be invited to compete. The proposal was approved unanimously and a committee constituted to draft the rules for the competition. Little could those present have realised that not only would their brainchild go on to become the pre-eminent sporting competition in England, it's concept would be copied across the entire globe.

Martin, Hall & Co. of Sheffield were then commissioned to create a trophy to be presented to the winners - the first cup being eighteen inches high and produced at a cost of £20.

The inaugural competition was something of an ad hoc affair, with most of the entrants being based in the Greater London area, within moderate travelling distance of Kennington Oval where the final was to be contested. The major exceptions being Queens Park of Glasgow and Donington School of Lincolnshire. These two were drawn together, but when Donington 'scratched' Queens Park were given a bye to the semi-final stage. Three of the original applicants, Harrow Chequers, Reigate Priory and the afore-mentioned Donington School withdrew without playing a game, so that only twelve clubs actually contested the issue: Barnes, Civil Service, Clapham Rovers, Crystal Palace, Hampstead Heathens, Hitchen, Maidenhead, Marlow, Royal Engineers, The Wanderers, Upton Park and Queens Park.

Queens Park withdrew after drawing their semi-final at the Oval when they lacked the funds to return for a replay. The Wanderers, a London based amateur club, were the first winners, beating the Royal Engineers by the only goal in the final at the Oval. It is perhaps appropriate that the first ever winners were captained by the very same C.W. Alcock that dreamed up the competition in the first place!

The Wanderers would go on to dominate the competition in it's early years, appearing in five of the first seven finals and winning the trophy on every occasion. In 1878 they won the cup for the third time, which, under the rules set forward by the F.A., made it their property outright. In a true spirit of sportsmanship, however, the Wanderers handed it back after the usual period of tenure, on condition that it should never again be won outright and always remain the property of the F.A.

Up to that time the F.A. Cup had remained a primarily southern competition. It was not until the 1880's, with the number of entrants growing each year and the ease of rail travel continuously improving, that it began to take on a more truly national complexion in terms of the geographic spread of the entrants. Indeed, the first northern winners were Blackburn Olympic, in 1882,

In 1886, the Blackburn Rovers emulated The Wanderers feat of a triple win, and since they could not keep the cup itself they were awarded a special trophy in recognition.

The original cup was used until 1895 when it was stolen from a shop in Birmingham. Aston Villa were then the holders, and had loaned the Cup to William Shillcock, one of their members and the proprietor of a prominent boot-maker and football outfitter's emporium in Newtown Row, Birmingham. Shillcock had displayed the trophy on a pedestal surrounded by a pile of football boots in the centre of his window display. When the store was opened at 8:00a.m. on Thursday 12th September, 1895, it was discovered that the premises had been broken into by thieves who had made a hole in the roof, and the valuable trophy stolen. It was never recovered, probably having been melted down for the scrap value of the silver of which it was made. Although the trophy was imposing in appearance, it was not very large, and the silver was thin so that it's scrap value not worth as much as the thieves may well have imagined – indeed, probably not more than the £10 offered as a reward for the cup's return. Aston Villa were subsequently fined £25 to pay for the manufacture of a replacement.

The new cup was used until 1910 after which it was replaced by a completely redesigned new model.

STRUCTURE OF THE COMPETITION

From the original 15 entrants for the Cup competition at it's inception in 1871 (the first final being played in 1872) by 1900 the number had now grown to well over 200! With only 32 teams required for the competition proper, to reduce by halves until reaching a final two, a preliminary and five qualifying rounds were staged to reduce the numbers, with the clubs being filtered in at various stages according to status.

The 22 top clubs, those being the previous season's semi-finalists and the best of the First Division clubs, all received a bye to the First Round proper. The rest competed in the qualifying competition for one of the remaining 10 places, filtering in at different stages according to status.

A Short History of Bury F.C.

Like many other football clubs, Bury's earliest origins can be traced back to the church. Changes to labour laws in the second half of the nineteenth century led to the common mill and/or factory worker, for the first time in history, having a regular Saturday afternoon of freedom. Initially this spare time was commonly spent in wanton activities like drinking and carousing, until, often with the encouragement of the church, sporting clubs began to arise to encourage the spending of this time in more wholesome activities.

In Bury, two such clubs were the Bury Wesleyans and Bury Unitarians Football Clubs, both of which can be traced back at least as far as 1876, at which time both were playing under rugby rules – the area then being a stronghold of the oval ball game. Over the ensuing years the Association code began to gain ground in the area, however, and by 1885 both of the aforementioned were operating under the alternate code (with the Unitarians at least seemingly running teams under both codes).

It was at this time that certain visionaries in the town began to dream of raising a first class Association club in the town, capable of playing at a higher level than any of the existing clubs in the town and competing against the best from across the county of Lancashire and beyond. To this end a series of meetings were held between the advocates of this plan, including representatives of both the Wesleyan and Unitarian clubs. These culminated in a historic meeting at the White Horse Hotel in Bury on April 24th, 1885, at which Bury F.C. was born.

From the start the new club played on the former Wesleyans' ground at Gigg Lane, the first game played by the new club however was away at nearby Little Lever, on September 5th, ending in a 0-0 draw. The first home game followed ten days later against a town club from Wigan. Bury scored three goals in the first half – a fourth on the stroke of half-time being disallowed as the referee had called time before it passed between the posts. Wigan hit back with their own trilogy in the second half but a further goal for the Buryites sealed the issue in their favour.

Bury entered the F.A. Cup for the first time in 1887 and their first tie was against Blackburn Rovers at Leamington Road (the Rover's ground). Bury scratched from the competition before the kick-off, however, and the match proceeded as an 'ordinary' one (this implies there being some obstacle to Bury's participation in a valid Cup tie – i.e. having travelled with one or more ineligible players – not a particularly unusual situation at the time). Bury lost the encounter 0-10!

Bury did not enter the F.A. Cup competition again until the 1891/92 when they were drawn at home to Witton in the 1st Qualifying round, gaining a 3-1 victory in front of 3000 supporters. Bury went on to defeat Heywood Central in the 2nd Qualifying round before bowing out to Blackpool in the 3rd after a replay. That same season, Bury won the Lancashire Senior Cup for the first time, defeating no less a side than cup giants Blackburn Rovers (three times F.A. Cup winners) in the final at Preston.

Common wisdom dictates that the club nickname, "the Shakers," was derived from an inspirational talk given by the club's chairman/manager John T. Ingham ahead of the Lancashire Senior Cup final on 25th April, 1892, when he uttered the phrase "We shall shake 'em. In fact we are the Shakers." However, the 'Cricket and Football Field' of January 9th, 1892, suggests that Ingham was perhaps paraphrasing an earlier usage from that journal which predates the latter event by four months! "'We will shake um,' says the Bury Shaker; and they did" - referring to the ordinary match against favourites Heywood Central in which Bury came back from a 1-2 half-time deficit to win 4-2. Thus whilst Ingham's usage may have popularised the name, there is no doubt it was already in existence.

In the meantime, Bury had become founder-members of the Lancashire League – from it's inception one of the strongest League's in the country and even considered a credible rival to the English League. In the first season of that competition, 1889/90, Bury finished runners-up, before going one better the following season and lifting the championship trophy. Bury retained the trophy the following season and only missed out on their third championship in a row the season after by the narrowest of margins – finishing only one point behind new champions Liverpool after drawing their final match at South Shore 1-1.

Bury finished runners-up to Blackpool in the Lancashire League championship at the end of the 1893/94 season but then beat the seasiders in the voting for election to the English Football League – gaining entry to that illustrious body whilst Blackpool were left behind. In their first season, Bury topped the Second Division table with a massive lead of nine points, then defeated First Division Liverpool in a promotion/relegation test match to trade places and earn a berth in the top flight.

Bury were then relative minnows in the company of big town and city clubs like Liverpool's Everton, Sheffield's United and Wednesday, Birmingham's Aston Villa, as well as the likes of Preston North End, Bolton Wanderers and Blackburn Rovers. But if the Shakers were lacking in resources they would quickly go on to show they lacked nothing in heart and/or fighting spirit, over the following seasons cementing their place among the Nation's best.

By 1900, however, after 15 years existence, the club was struggling with crippling long-term debt's and in very real danger of folding. It was only the proceeds of a hugely successful five day bazaar (22nd-26th February, 1900) that kept the club afloat - not only clearing the debts but even providing additional funds to begin much needed improvements at Gigg Lane.

In the hope of a good Cup run to further bolster the club's finances the Directors had previously instituted a bonus of £1 a man for a Cup tie victory. Having progressed to the Third Round this was now raised to £5 a man, and the tie at Sheffield taking place on the third day of the bazaar news of the play, received by telegraph, was announced at ten minute intervals.

Few could yet have realised, just how far Bury were destined to go in the competition or that the club's finest hour was so close around the corner!

The Climate of the Time

The 1899/1900 season had begun as normal, but by Christmas the game was in the doldrums, with attendances well down from their usual levels and a general level of apathy among supporters that frequently affected the players on the field.

The reason for this was was that Great Britain was, at the time, at War! In 1880, British attempts to annexe the Transvaal in South Africa had met with armed resistance from the Dutch colonists, the Trekboers, leading to the First Boer War (December 1880 – March 1881). It was a short but bloody conflict, ending in a treaty by which the Boers were permitted to maintain self-government whilst surrendering to British suzerainty.

It was an uneasy peace, however, and war broke out again in October 1899. This time the Boers were much better prepared, and in the early stages inflicted several costly reverses on the British forces. The garrison towns of Ladysmith, Mafeking, Kimberley were surrounded and laid under siege, trapping thousands of British soldiers inside, whilst elsewhere the well-armed and highly mobile Boers outmanoeuvred and defeated British armies at Colenso, Magersfontein and Stormberg. The British forces had been taken completely by surprise and for a time it seemed that the greatly outnumbered Boers might even win.

Lancs Fusiliers marching to the relief of Ladysmith

All of this had a profound effect on the mood at home. The nation was gripped by the plight of the besieged towns - eager to read the next of the reports that constantly filled the newspapers. The Government, meanwhile, reacted by calling up thousands of reservists[2] to send to the aid of the beleaguered British colonial forces and begin the fight back.

Consequently, with thousands of men gone away to fight, and the hearts and minds of those at home diverted by the conflict, from where the early news had nearly all been bad, interest in football had waned considerably, with huge drops in attendances at matches all across the country. In few places was this more heartfelt than Lancashire, with the county's own Lancashire Regiment being at the very forefront of the fightback.

It wasn't until the following spring, when that fight back had begun, the besieged towns were each in their turn relieved, and the Boers driven back by defeat after defeat that the mood at home lifted and things started getting back to normal.

---

2   There was no general conscription so the playing staffs of the professional clubs were largely unaffected.

1899/1900 - The First Round

At the time only 32 teams were entered into the competition 'proper', starting at the First Round. These consisted of:
a. *The four semi-finalists from the previous season's competition.*
b. *Fifteen sides selected from the English League.*
c. *Three sides selected from the Southern League.*
d. *The ten survivors of a qualifying competition through which all other entrants had to progress.*

Bury entered the competition at this stage as one of the seeded League sides, as did reigning their eventual Cup final opponents, Southern League champions Southampton, as one of that League's representatives.

Bury were comfortably expected to overcome their struggling First Division rival's Burnley, but Southampton looked to have a mammoth job on their hands to get by another First Division side – Everton, one of the richest clubs of the era. With the particular exception of Notts County's 6-0 defeat of Chorley, scoring on the day was unusually low, with ten of the sixteen sides involved, like Chorley, failing to score at all.

BURNLEY v. BURY
at Turf Moor, Burnley – Saturday 27th January, 1900
Athletic News - Monday 27th January, 1900
A HARD STRUGGLE AT BURNLEY
[By Turf Moor]

Burnley could have had only slight hopes of pulling off their tie with Bury on Saturday. In the first place, although the Turf Moorites had choice of ground, they had to encounter what is admittedly one of the best teams going just now. Sheffield United, I dare say, will admit that much. In the second place the "reds" were very unfortunately situated with regard to their players. Hartley and Hannigan, who have played in cup ties for Woolwich Arsenal, were ineligible, while Place, junior, was suffering from injuries, and in so tight a corner did the directors find themselves with regard to the selection of the forward line that they did not finally decide on the composition of the team until shortly before the match. It was then found necessary to impress into service the veteran Place, senior, and that in the position of outside right, while Bowes was essayed the role of centre forward. Bury were fortunate in having their full team available. Neither side had indulged in the luxury of seaside training quarters, contenting themselves with careful preparation at home. After so much rain as we have had recently the going was necessarily heavy, and things were not improved by the mixture of snow and rain that came down during Saturday morning. Nor were the "gate" receipts improved thereby. The outlook all through the morning was anything but promising, and must have tended to seriously diminish the attendance. The actual receipts were £178 9s. 9d., which represents an attendance of nearly 7000, and of those a considerable number hailed from Bury.

Hillman won the toss, and set Bury to start up the slope against a rather lively breeze. Burnley were the first to get going, but it was not long before the Bury forwards made a move. Then a spell of even play ensued, following which Burnley inaugurated a warm attack on the visitors' goal, and, aided by the wind, they remained for some time in the Bury quarters. Bowes was fouled while shooting, and from the ensuing free kick Edgar Chadwick experienced hard lines. The Bury forwards were always on the lookout for opportunities, and did not fail to put them to good use. On one occasion McLuckie got right in front of Hillman, but the latter saved his charge in characteristic style. On neither side did the forward play afternoon attain to a high degree of excellence, the play being quite of the usual Cup tie order. Generally, the defence had distinctly the best of it. The Bury rear division had plenty of work to do, but nothing came amiss to them. At the other end Hillman and his backs also had a fair amount of occupation, and they came well out of the ordeal, the custodian especially. Burnley were more frequently in their opponents' half, but the forwards could not penetrate the Bury defence, and at half time there was no score.

In the second half it was expected that Bury would have much the best of the argument, but this did not turn out to be the case, and for some time Burnley fully held their own. It looked all up once when Sagar crossing over to the right wing, took a pass from Richards, and raced clean away, but Hillman, with a splendid effort, just tipped his shot over the bar. An almost equally fine shot by Morrison at the other end was cleared by Thompson, and he repeated the operation soon afterwards from Barron. Play had proceeded about twenty-five minutes when, from a centre by Miller, Bowes headed the ball into the net, amid loud cheers. The jubilation was short-lived however, for the referee, after consulting Mr. Cooper, of Blackburn, one of the linesman, disallowed the point on the ground that Miller was offside. It was certainly a very fine point as to whether he was offside or not, and the referee at first seemed to incline to the idea that it was a legitimate goal, as he commenced to walk to the centre of the field, but noticing Mr. Cooper's signal he turned back and pointed for a free kick, to the intense disappointment of the home side - players and spectators alike. A few minutes later Bury scored what proved to be the only goal of the match, **Sagar** netting the ball from close quarters, from Richard's pass, Hillman having no chance. From now the visitors had the best of matters, Burnley having evidently become disheartened and Wood nearly added to the score with a shot that struck one of the uprights and rebounded into play. No further goals resulted, however, and Bury retired winners by a goal to nil.

On the day's play one cannot but hesitate about affirming that the winners were the better side. The disorganised Burnley front rank did much better than was expected of them, and they certainly made the pace warm for the opposing defence. It was unfortunate that the home side should have to take the field at so serious a disadvantage, but that, of course, was not the fault of their opponents on Saturday. The match may be described as a typical Cup-tie. One missed the fine touches that are ordinarily looked for, but on the other hand there was plenty of vigour displayed, and notwithstanding the heavy going, both sides stayed well. Burnleyites were very much dissatisfied with the decision which negatived their goal, and especially with the circumstances under which the point was disallowed. I did not notice Mr. Brodie blow his whistle, giving Miller offside, when he first played the ball. There was no doubt about the point secured by Bury, though it looked as though one of the Burnley defenders ought just to have prevented Sagar getting in his shots. Perhaps, under all the circumstances, Burnley deserved a draw, and with their crippled team they would have been satisfied with that. The defence, as I have intimated, outshone the attack on both sides. The two goalkeepers came out of the ordeal with great credit, and both sets of backs and halves put in excellent work. The forwards seemed to rely principally on rushing tactics, and in the absence of science they displayed any amount of vigour.

RESULT: Burnley 0 – Bury 1

BURY: Thompson (goal); Darroch and Davidson (backs); Pray, Leeming and Ross (halves); Richards, Wood, McLuckie, Sagar [1] and Plant (forwards).
BURNLEY: Hillman (goal); Woolfall and McLintock (backs); Barron, Taylor and Livingston (halves); Place snr., Morrison, Bowes, Chadwick and Miller (forwards).
Referee: Mr. Brodie (Wolverhampton)

SOUTHAMPTON v. EVERTON
at the Dell, Southampton – Saturday 27th January, 1900
Athletic News - Monday 27th January, 1900
DOWNFALL OF EVERTON
[By Ants]

{Warning – as a historical record the following report is reproduced verbatim but contains a word and an allusion that may now be considered racially offensive.}

Shocking weather prevailed at Southampton on Saturday, and had there been much more rain play would have been seriously endangered. As it was, the spectators were nothing like as numerous as was expected, the attendance being about 10,000. The players, too, had to put up with a lot of discomfort and play on a pitch that was at times very slippery, and all through the game very heavy. The Everton team did not arrive in Southampton till shortly before the match, having broken the long journey at Winchester. The Southampton men have done their training locally, taking spins in the new forest. Except that T. Farrell was still weak from influenza, both teams were at full strength, and looked remarkably fit.

Everton won the toss, but what wind there was blew across the ground, and indeed was little felt in the deep hollow of the Dell. That there was little advantage in choice was shown by the fact that the ball almost invariably landed more than halfway when kicked off from either end. Soon after the rain began to fall, and continued for more than half an hour. From the rush up Milward almost immediately netted the ball, but was ruled offside. Of the two elevens Southampton started off smarter, and had considerably the best of matters for a time, Blythe, who received a nasty kick, but refused to retire, being the most conspicuous in Everton's ranks. Several shots reached Muir, but none gave any difficulty. The Saints tactics seemed superior, the Everton forwards playing rather wildly. Settle tried a long ground shot, but Robinson easily saved. Proudfoot kicked over the bar, and at the other end Muir had great trouble with a curling shot by Turner. Southampton were distinctly pressing, and on one occasion all but scored from a free kick close up. At this stage of the game Balmer and Eccles were very active, and repeatedly saved the situation. Rain had now ceased, and for a time the sun shone out brightly, but the surface was extremely sticky, and it is a wonder the players kept their feet as well as they did. There were no pools on the ground, but a thick coating of mud in large areas may play very hard. Robinson saved a fine shot by Proudfoot, but danger seldom came near the Saints goal, whereas Muir was called on four times in little more than a minute to save. A skirmishing run by Everton's left gave Proudfoot what seemed an easy chance, but he kicked wide. Towards half-time Everton began to recover, or, perhaps, to put it nicely, to gain the upper hand, and forced two corners, but found the defence very sound, Meehan's powerful kicks frequently landing the ball well back in their own half of the ground.

Half-time came with no score, and from the improvement Everton showed in smartness and dash the game looked likely to end in their favour. Right away from the kick off Robinson had to catch a very hot shot; then Abbot just missed by inches, and three corners fell to Everton, and the least slice of luck at this point might have entirely changed the aspect of the whole game, as it was some time before Southampton got going again. Meston opened a retaliating attack with a curling shot that Muir only just reached, but Everton, working with great determination, forced the play back. Abbot's work at left half being very noticeable, Proudfoot missed the opportunity of the day, as, with an open goal, in consequence of Durber slipping, he shot against the side of the net. A better directed shot would probably have meant a win for Everton. It seemed to be the turning point of the game, for after nearly half an hour's play, during which the visitors had decidedly overpowered Southampton and lost several chances, the Saints began to wake up, and pushed their attacks hard. Farrell and Wood both tested Muir, and it began to look as if the Saints would have to visit the Mersey to replay, when a stroke of luck came their way. From a free kick some distance up the field, the ball landed in front of goal, and **Milward** clumsily but effectively diverted it into the net. The enthusiasm displayed around the ground proved what a relief that goal was to the locals, but when from the kick off the Saints were seen to be hanging back in the defence with a whole quarter of an hour yet to play, while Everton strove desperately to equalise, the situation began to look grave indeed. Abbott, Settle, Gray, and Taylor were conspicuous for dashing play. It was a clear case of neck or nothing with Everton, but strive as they would the ball only once reached Robinson, when he fell down with it. For a moment there was almost dead silence as the International held the ball from three or four opponents. Then it slipped out of his hands, but luckily for Southampton Durber kicked away. It was a most exciting time when the referee gave a free kick against Meehan for jumping at Taylor close up, but this attack also failed. Proudfoot, who had signally bad luck, missed, by a hair's breadth, from another free kick. Then Milward and Farrell took the ball down. Milward tricked Eccles, and centring, **Turner**, with a steadily aimed shot, scored a second goal. This settled the game for there was only four minutes more to play, but in that short time the Saints revelled in attack, and quite ran round their opponents, and from a corner kick **Milward** headed the third goal close on time, Southampton winning by three to none.

It was a hard fought game, and taken all through Southampton deserved their win, but they were not three goals superior. At the same time, it must be remembered that while Muir had to save on many occasions, Robinson had very little to do. Some of Muir's saves were lucky, but Everton missed several goals by the merest shade of the goal posts, any one of which would probably have settled the Saints. Generally speaking, there was more speed and method in the winner's forward five than in their opponents, who seemed very much at sea. Settle who is always expected to go great things, did very little, Meehan being quite as fast and weighing two stone more, giving the International anything but a rosy time of it; in fact, speed did not seem to be a great point with Everton, and in striking contrast was Turner's brilliant runs on Southampton's right and Milward's quick work on the left. Turner, who a year ago, was a local junior, is without doubt one of the best of forwards, and the cool and confident manner in which he scored his goal was worthy of a Goodall. In defence, Everton appeared to have the advantage at half, where Blythe and Abbott worked like niggers, but Southampton's backs, Durber and Meehan shone in front of Eccles and Balmer, though Eccles was very sound. It was Meehan's day out, and excepting his rather erratic kicking at times, he was in fine form. It is not unjust to Everton to express the opinion that on the day's play Southampton were a percentage smarter, and certainly faster. Choice of ground, of course, made a great difference, probably that between defeat and the second round of the cup, but as a team the Saints on no ground would be inferior to their opponents. Their victory gave intense satisfaction to Hampshire people, and it would not be easy for Everton to explain away so heavy a defeat, for the defence distinctly broke down in the last fifteen minutes.

RESULT: Southampton 3 – Everton 0

SOUTHAMPTON: Robinson (goal); Durber and Meehan (backs); Petrie, Chadwick and Meston (halves); Turner [1], Yates, Farrell, Wood and Milward [2] (forwards).
EVERTON: Muir (goal); Balmer and Eccles (backs); Abbott, Blythe and Wolstenholme (halves); Gray, Settle, Proudfoot, Taylor and Sharp (forwards).
Referee: Mr. Brodie (Wolverhampton)

OTHER RESULTS

27th January, 1900

Bristol City	2–1	Stalybridge Rovers
Derby County	2–2	Sunderland
Jarrow	0–2	**Millwall Athletic**
Manchester City	1–1	Aston Villa
Newcastle United	2–1	Reading
Nottingham Forest	3–0	Grimsby Town
Notts County	6–0	Chorley
Queens Park Rangers	1–1	Wolverhampton Wanderers
Portsmouth	0–0	Blackburn Rovers
Preston North End	1–0	Tottenham Hotspur
Stoke	0–0	Liverpool
Sheffield United	1–0	Leicester Fosse
The Wednesday	1–0	Bolton Wanderers
Walsall	1–1	West Bromwich Albion

31st January, 1900

Aston Villa	3–0	Manchester City
Sunderland	3–0	Derby County
Wolverhampton Wanderers	0–1	**Queens Park Rangers**

1st February 1900   Blackburn Rovers 1–1 Portsmouth
                                      Liverpool 1–0 Stoke
                    West Bromwich Albion 6–1 Walsall

5th February 1900   **Blackburn Rovers** 5–0 Portsmouth

1899/1900 - The Second Round

In an era when the North and Midlands dominated the football scene, the South had been provided a considerable fillip by the performances of the Southern League clubs that had taken part in the First Round Proper of the national cup competition. Bristol City and Millwall had both advanced, albeit against relatively weak Northern sides, but more importantly, besides Southampton's hugely surprising win over Everton, Queen's Park Rangers had achieved, if anything, an even bigger shock by turning over high-flying Wolverhampton Wanderers after a replay, whilst Portsmouth had held cup battlers Blackburn Rovers to a second replay before succumbing.

With the second round draw placing Millwall and Queens Park Rangers in internecine conflict at least one southern club was guaranteed to proceed further whilst Southampton's luck in being drawn at home again to a strong Newcastle United outfit gave them at least a credible chance of being a second, whereas Bristol City were surely lambs to the slaughter at League leaders Aston Villa.

Sheffield would be a city divided with their two clubs, United and Wednesday, pitted in conflict whilst the denizens of Nottingham would be spoilt for choice with both their sides having plum ties at home, Forest entertaining Sunderland whilst the County club welcomed Bury!

NOTTS. COUNTY v. BURY
at Trent Bridge, Nottingham – Saturday 10th February, 1900
Athletic News - Monday 12th February, 1900
BURY IN LUCK'S WAY [By Nondescript]

Nottingham must have been favoured by the Gods on Saturday. To judge by the reports when one arrived home at night it seems to have been snowing in nearly every other town in Britain. It is not for me to ask whether there should have been any reason for such special dispensation, but what I do know is that we at the office do hereby state solemnly and on oath that we are under great obligation to Nottingham this morning for being able to issue a sheet consisting of something more than house advertisements, and the coupons and extracts from esteemed contemporaries, and that two fellow voyagers who crossed the Withy-grove drift a few minutes before closing time offered up a devout thanksgiving that they had been so far and been able to see so much. Ah! I have it. When I come to think of it, my cheery travelling companion who spreads himself over another column was carrying with him all the appurtenances for warning off snow for miles round the Trent Valley. He had a red face, glowing with the prospect of visiting his native land once more; a red tie, a red kerchief, a red-striped dickie – I'm hanged if he wasn't vermilion hued down to the covers of his pocketbook. For he was a Forester bold, you see. Our ways parted at Gamston-lane and I joined the glad throng that went laughing along to the old familiar pitch on the cricket ground, where Notts. and Bury gave us an entertainment which for real fun and genuine excitement I'll warrant beat anything the opposition was able to produce. From all accounts they had the bigger crowd nearer the river, for there was plenty of room and good seeing at our show. I always think that cut and dried details of a Saturday's game, even a Cup tie, are the least acceptable portion of one's notes book, especially when it is opened two days after the event. In this case, however, I intend to allow myself a little more rope than usual. If the idea does not commend itself from a reader's point of view, it will, at any rate, assist the editor in filling up an aching void. He is a gentleman who gets the paper out. And then the folks at Bury will want to know something about the affair, for though odd chunks of Lancashire dialect flattened themselves against the sharp pointed wintry air in various corners of the ground, Bury shouters were very few. Story of goals? God bless you, sirs. I'm like the needy knife grinder and have none to tell, but I can say that we are always expecting them, even to the last few minutes. The signalling apparatus from the other side of Gamston-lane was working overtime compared with that hoisted on the cricket ground. We never once had an opportunity of waving an answer back over the house stops. But I expect we saw more fight on our little plot. As might have been imagined, the ground was as hard as a board, and such light fleecy carpeting as there was on top, whilst it afforded no protecting cushion for a fellow who capsized, contributed to such a series of vagaries on the part of both man and ball that we were never wearied in so waiting patiently to the end for something tangible to turn up.

It was some time ere Notts. got warm, so to speak. Bury had the wind, and for a quarter of an hour or so opened up some very threatening attacks on the home goal. Several beautiful centres from their left wing, chiefly on the part of Sagar, gave those on the other side of the field at least two grand chances, and had Richards been able to get his shot in on one occasion it might - but then he slipped, so it is no use hazarding an opinion as to what might have been. Another time the same forwards banged over the top with an opening quite as good. Hampered as they were with a frisky ball, which very often beat the players itself, such "side" as it was able to take, and conditions which frequently led to them floundering about, and describing all sorts of angles with the earth, the Bury men showed some remarkably fine football in these early stages, Sagar leading the way in great style, and though Notts. gradually found their feet and the way to the other end the visitors were doing rather the better work. Theirs, however, was the goal which had the first narrow escape of being captured, for after a scurry on the Notts. right had led to a melee in front of the posts McMain banged the ball in for all he was worth. Unfortunately, it struck the bar - Thompson was all over beaten - and worse still for the Notts. man, while he was in the act of taking the rebound Davidson went for him full tilt, and catching him on one leg sent him sprawling. He was "outed" for the moment, and had to be helped off the field, the while the crowd were shrieking their hardest for a penalty. There was, as far as I could see, no call for the utmost severity of the law. It was a heavy charge certainly, and the Notts. man, caught unawares, had no alternative but to go flying headlong. What incensed the Notts. partisans, however, was that while the referee passed the incident over - as in my estimation he was perfectly right in doing - he failed to see McMain lying prone on the ground, and allowed play to progress towards the other end of the field before his attention was arrested. And, as on other occasions during the afternoon, Mr. Armitt missed several little points, the people bore him a full-sized grudge for the remainder of the day. As often happens, it was his duty to have to penalise Notts. once or twice immediately after this incident, and - well, you know how a crowd behaves under these circumstances. Later on a fine shot by Maconnachie tried the Bury defence, and it was sorely bothered by some well judged returns from Lewis, who seemed to have got the range to a nicety. At the other end came a ball from Plant slick at the bar, and then at the Bury backs, who had been kicking stoutly, prepared to receive cavalry at the Gamston-lane goal, full of the knowledge that against the breeze in the second half they would have a much busier time.

It was so, for in the last forty-five minutes Notts. had the best of the argument in midfield. Play had not progressed long after the interval ere the notion gained that Bury had decided to adopt a Boer-like like attitude, and entrench themselves for the rest of the game. First Sagar, who had been the star artist among the forwards, began to hang back, and gradually the forward work was left to Plant on the right wing, the others having a pop every now and then, but generally getting rid of the ball without much heed as to where it was going. There may be some good argument for these tactics, which once sees employed frequently with League teams, but they have never convinced me. You take a forward off and play him half-back, and a half-back puts himself a sort of three-quarter, and if you call this a strengthening of the defence I must respectfully beg to differ with you. It is a strengthening which gives the opposition attack all the more scope, and here the Notts. backs and halves were able to enjoy a good deal of elbow room, while those on the other side were frequently in each other's way. A bungle between Sagar and McLuckie, for instance, led to Hadley speeding off, and putting in a centre, which found the Bury defence all at sixes and sevens, with the result that Thompson came out, dived in to the thick of the melee, and managed to break the ball away at the feet of Maconnachie. Had the latter taken in the situation he would have dribbled a few paces away from the ruck and found an open and tenantless goal, but instead he fired from the spot, and was too high. Of course the Bury forwards, in twos and threes, several times reached the pavilion end. Plant once brought Suter to his knees, the custodian showing his resource by whisking the ball round the post. But Notts. were the more dangerous, and it was desperately hard luck when a beautiful cross shot from Chalmers put the ball to the far corner of the net a second or so after the referee had signalled a free kick. Again when the same forward was tripped by Pray in the last 2 minutes, the incident took place inches only away from the penalty line, and if I were to say that fate came to the rescue of the Lancastrians I should be hurting no one's feelings.

Still Bury are entitled to all the credit, as I was led to believe that Notts. were an improved team. It didn't require much for them to beat the form I saw when last at the Bridge: still, they did beat it, without, I should imagine, giving their friends anything like full satisfaction. Ball for instance, was very weak, and as a result the Bury left wing were able to make a good deal of dangerous running, though I imagine that Plant and Sagar would have bothered any defence on Saturday, and they were the best wing on the ground. Ball however, worked like a Trojan throughout, and it was chiefly owing to his vigilance that McLuckie was not so conspicuous as usual. Ball is a regular "knight of the rueful countenance," serious in everything he does, and nearly always in the vicinity of the ball. In this particular I should say that Notts. certainly are an improved team. Weakness on the left wing, noticeable a month or two back, has also been rectified, and Chalmers seems to have outlived hostile criticism. He is somewhat slow in gathering a ball, but, like the broker's man, very useful when in possession. His shot was a beauty; better I thought, then any of those which struck the bar or the posts - and it was real hard luck that it was prevented from counting. Other worthies on the home side entitled to mention are Hadley, who as a rule made the most of his opportunities, and Lewis, who until the time when he fell awkwardly played with remarkable strength. From a defensive point of view, however, nothing was finer than the display of Darroch and Davidson, who, considering how treacherous the ground was, made mistakes so few that they could easily be counted on your fingers. They timed their men remarkably well, and broke up many an attack which threatened danger, although it must be said that the Notts. inside forwards frequently sold themselves to the enemy. Such times as the Bury attack had the full complement of men out doing work it was a much better affair, though it was weak rather on the right. The halves played strongly all the way through, but as I have said, the main idea, apparently, of the visitors after the interval was to wait on their opponents, and their play was not nearly so spicy. There was little in it taking the game on the whole, but to my mind Notts., apart from the ill-luck they experienced, missed their way, and should have had no occasion for travelling to Gigg-lane tomorrow. Bury of course, appreciate the move to the home quarters, for this is the Second English cup tie, I believe, they have had in their midst for five years. I think now they will get through with it.

RESULT: Notts. County 0 – Bury 0

BURY: Thompson (goal); Darroch and Davidson (backs); Pray, Leeming and Ross (halves); Richards, Wood, McLuckie, Sagar and Plant (forwards).
NOTTS. COUNTY: Suter (goal); Lewis and Montgomery (backs); Ball, Bull and McDonald (halves); Hadley, Maconnachie, McMain, Goss and Chalmers (forwards).
Referee: Mr. T. Armitt (Leeds)

BURY v. NOTTS. COUNTY (Replay)
At Gigg Lane, Bury – Wednesday 14th February, 1900.
Nottingham Evening Post - Wednesday 14th February, 1900
BURY v. NOTTS [By Nondescript]

Admittedly, Notts. were the victims of sheer misfortune in having to journey to Bury today for the purpose of replaying their tie with the Gigg-laners in the second round of the competition for the Association Cup. Even allowing for the fact that in the first encounter at Trent Bridge they had fallen far short of the standard they have shown of late in the League, they nevertheless deserved to win on the play, and exasperating luck was, after all, the prime factor in bringing them face to face with an ordeal which few teams in the country would tackle successfully. In their favour it could be urged that little more than a month ago they had beaten the present champions of Lancashire on their own ground, but since that time Bury have earned the distinction of being the first to defeat the League leaders, and notwithstanding the former success it has been a desperately hard struggle for any team to secure spoils at Gigg-lane this season. All things considered the Bury club have been capably and consistently represented throughout the campaign, and the qualities of dash and determination so essential to success in Cup ties have been the distinguishing characteristics of the side in pretty well all their engagements. Encouraged by the result of their visit to Trent Bridge the men made no secret of their confidence in the ultimate issue of the replayed match, and their keen desire for victory was not lessened by the reflection that five years had lapsed since they had had the opportunity of contesting a Cup tie on their own ground. The visitors on the other hand, were spurred on to a supreme effort by the knowledge that if they emerged successfully from the struggle they would be sharers in a lucrative gate at one or other of the Sheffield grounds, and in spite of the fact that appearances were on the whole in favour of the home team, the players themselves were exceedingly hopeful of confirming the results of their previous visit. From every point of view the game promised to be intensely exciting, and the only regret felt was that it could not be decided on a Saturday, with the prospect of a very much larger attendance. Originally it had been decided that the teams should meet on Tuesday, but a heavy snowstorm in Lancashire rendered it necessary to postpone it for another day, and even this morning the outlook, when the Notts. players left home, accompanied by some of the directors, was none too promising. The men did not return to Hazleford after the match on Saturday, but trained quietly in Nottingham, and were in the best of spirits when they entered upon their journey by the Midland Railway at five minutes past nine. There was a very heavy fall of snow during the night at Bury but the ground had been admirably cleared. Sand was strewn over the turf, but it was very slippery on the surface, and exceedingly hard beneath. The afternoon was beautifully fine, but the gate did not exceed 4,000. There was no change in the home team.

Pray won the toss, and Bury had the sun at their backs in the first half, but there was nothing else in the conditions to favour either side. Early on Sagar fed McLuckie with excellent judgement, but Montgomery stepped in and cleared, and after smart work by the Notts. forwards, Chalmers ran the ball over the line. McMain was applauded for pretty play in midfield, but his final pass to Hadley went out, and the game was then temporarily suspended through an injury to Ball, who was kicked in the face by Wood. Sturdy tackling by Pray set the home forwards on the move, but Montgomery and Lewis forced them back, and, Hadley being allowed to run in from an offside position, Darroch headed out a likely shot, while Ball placed wide. McMain was penalised for charging Pray in the back, and McDonald for holding Richards, but neither free kick was improved upon, and Notts. racing to the other end, McDonald had bad luck with a beautiful shot, which grazed the upright. At the Notts. end Sagar, from an awkward angle, made an equally meritorious attempt, but the ball sailed over the bar, and a speedy burst by the Notts. right caused Thomson to fist out from Hadley, though the shot presented little difficulty. End to end exchanges followed, but Bury gradually worked down, and Pray and Darroch forced successive corners, Suter making a feeble clearance on the first occasion. "Hands" against Darroch enabled Notts. to relieve, and Maconnachie from long range shot past, Montgomery repelling Pray's effort. Ball was pulled up for holding Plant, but nothing came of the free kick, and though McLuckie fed Sagar beautifully, he lost possession to Montgomery, and a flying shot by Leeming went over the bar. In the next moment, Plant, neatly fed by Ross, sent across a pretty centre, which Richards took in the corner of the goal, but his shot luckily went out of danger. Pretty passing by the Notts. forwards transferred play, and the home goal escaped downhill in miraculous fashion from both Goss and MaConnachie. Ultimately Chalmers forced a corner, and here from Plant raced down the field with a clean course. Tricking Lewis, he shot hard and straight at goal, but the ball cannoned off the Notts. right back to Suter, and Chalmers missed a capital chance by failing to screw when all his colleagues were well in front. A misunderstanding between Lewis and Montgomery left McLuckie with almost an open goal, but his shot went wide, and Wood just after was given offside. Thomson caught and threw away a smart shot from Chalmers, and McMain made a capital attempt to convert a pretty centre by Hadley, but the ball rolled past the post. Notts. were now holding the upper hand, and, Davidson slipping, Hadley raced up to goal, but shot wide just when the score seemed imminent, while McMain sent past. The visitors then had a narrow escape from Plant. Half-time:- Notts. nil; Bury nil

When hostilities were resumed Notts. immediately rushed down, and from a centre by Hadley Goss had the chance of the match with only Thomson to beat at five yards range, but he shot straight into the keeper's hands, the escape of the Bury goal being greeted with huge delight. And the home forwards were not long in returning the compliment, but Richards slipped upon the treacherous turf, and McDonald relieved. A moment later Plant centred into the goalmouth, and Montgomery and McDonald both fell, but Wood lost the opening. Better success attended the home side directly after, however, for **Sagar**, securing close in, ran through the defence, and gave Suter no possible chance with a shot which opened the scoring after three and a half minutes. The visitors had an opportunity of equalising within a minute, with four of the forwards right in front of goal, but Hadley misdirected. Free kicks either way for imaginary fouls created intense amusement among the crowd, who were now on good terms with themselves, and the whistle pulled McMain up for offside when the visiting centre was well placed. Richards sent across a fine centre, which Plant met, and the ball fell on Wood's toe almost on the line, but the inside right could only clear the bar by yards just as Ball knocked him over. Bury were now having distinctly the best of the exchanges, and Darroch twice placed the ball beautifully in the goalmouth, but Montgomery cleared in gallant style, and on the second occasion the ball bounced off the bar on to the top of the net. Then for a while play opened up, but MacDonald was penalised for jumping, and the Notts. defence was again sorely tried. Wood, however, lost a splendid chance, and Leeming shot widely in the course of another attack. Plant was hurt, but continued to play, and Bury coming again with rare dash, shot after shot was put in at the Notts. goal. For a second or so it seemed destined to escape the downfall, but **Pray**, meeting the ball from a rebound, made no mistake, and placed his side still further ahead after a quarter of an hour. Notts. were at this stage playing the beaten game, and Suter had to fist out a fine long shot from Pray, while Wood misdirected after a promising run. Hadley at length relieved, and Thomson tipped over the bar a glorious shot from McDonald, the corner being quite futile. Ball was penalised for tripping McLuckie, and Davidson by putting his knee into Maconnachie's chest, but neither free kick was improved upon, and Suter cleared from Sagar. A miskick by Ross let Hadley through, but his centre dropped behind. The visitors were showing wretched form in every department hereabouts, and play was all in favour of Bury, who pressed heavily in the hope of augmenting their lead.

RESULT: Bury 2 - Notts. County 0

BURY: Thompson (goal); Darroch and Davidson (backs); Pray [1], Leeming and Ross (halves); Richards, Wood, McLuckie, Sagar [1] and Plant (forwards).
NOTTS. COUNTY: Suter (goal); Lewis and Montgomery (backs); Ball, Bull and McDonald (halves); Hadley, Maconnachie, McMain, Goss and Chalmers (forwards).
Referee: Mr. T. Armitt (Leeds)

SOUTHAMPTON v. NEWCASTLE UNITED
at the Dell, Southampton – Saturday 10th February, 1900
Athletic News - Monday 12th February, 1900
NEWCASTLE'S HARD LINES [By Hants]

Nobody can gainsay the fact that Newcastle had extremely hard luck in their cup tie at Southampton on Saturday, though, of course, the Saints suffered a sad misfortune in an accident which lost them their centre forward, Farrell. For Newcastle to have to play the full half match against a blinding snowstorm, and then when they appeared to have the game in their hands for the match to be abandoned five minutes after the restart, is what I mean when I head this report "Newcastle's hard lines." As far as the game had gone up to the stoppage Newcastle had shown themselves distinctly the cleverer team, and the better equal to play under the disadvantages of the day. It is just two years ago that the luck of the draw compelled Newcastle, then a coming and ambitious second-rate club, to visit Southampton, and the Saints won a hard game by one goal to none. Since then Newcastle have taken top rank and made a much quicker improvement than the Saints, who in that memorable year for the South reached the semi-final tie. It is probable that Southampton are a little better side than in 1898, but not much. Newcastle's form away from home has been so consistently good that it was felt as soon as the draw came out that Southampton would need to go all the way, and that their chief hope to win lay in having secured choice of ground. The United broke the long journey by going as far as Winchester on Wednesday, and wisely put in a little training there near Southampton. Peddie's return to the forward rank strengthened their attack, and the team was at full strength. The same may be said of the Saints, who trained in the New Forest, finding that method did so well against Everton. The severe frost which commenced on Wednesday began by its continuance to threaten the possibility of play, but on Friday night the weather changed and a thaw set in. It was, however, very slight, and yet it was sufficient to enable Mr. Kingscott, the referee, who travelled overnight from Derby to allow the game to proceed. The ground was hard, but being well grassed was from all appearances playable. And that was my opinion also at midday. The attendance was very good considering, being close on 10,000.

The opening stages of the game at once showed up the pace of the Newcastle men who, in spite of the hard surface, displayed a very smart play and kept their feet better than the locals. A short experience of the ground showed that the estimate of its fitness was hardly borne out by results, for at the best the players had great difficulty in keeping their feet, and there were frequent spills. Newcastle threatened the Saints goal for a long time, though snow had begun to fall and drifted thickly into their faces. Almost the only decent bit of work by the Saints in the first 10 minutes was a grand shot by Chadwick, and generally speaking they showed up badly in face of the superior tactics of their opponents, and one began to wonder what had happened to the side since their victory over Everton. At times they fared better, but when after about twenty minutes play Farrell fell heavily and was taken off with his shoulder put out, Southampton's hopes fell to zero. Still, up to half-time play was pretty even; but the snow falling heavily had covered the ground with a sheet of white, and made the surface as slippery again, and at any minute it was expected that the game would be stopped.

However, the players came out again after the usual rest, and after a consultation play recommenced. In the first 5 minutes several slips and falls occurred, and it really became clear that play was not only getting dangerous but a farce. The Newcastle men were not anxious to stop, holding all the trumps in their hands so to speak, but accepted the referee's decision to abandon the game in good spirit. The crowd made no demonstration, but quietly left the ground. It would be unfair to criticise the players beyond saying that so far as it went Newcastle made a grand show, and looked a winning team. They seemed more at home and would doubtless have won. The Saints were playing very much below form, and must consider themselves lucky in the match ending abruptly after they had failed to score with the snow at their backs. D. Gardner, Higgins, Peddie, and McFarlane showed up prominently on the Newcastle side, Higgins particularly, while Chadwick stood out conspicuously in the Saints team, and Durber and Turner were also in good form.

ABANDONED: Southampton 0 - Newcastle United 0

SOUTHAMPTON: Robinson (goal); Durber and Meehan (backs); Petrie, Chadwick and Meston (halves); Turner, Yates, Farrell, Wood and Milward (forwards).
NEWCASTLE UTD: Kingsley (goal); D. Gardner and Aitken (backs); Carr, Higgins and Ghee (halves); Fraser, McFarlane, Peddie, Stevenson and A. Gardner (forwards).
Referee: Mr. A. Kingscott (Derby)

SOUTHAMPTON v. NEWCASTLE UNITED (Replay)
At the Dell, Southampton – 17th February, 1900.
Athletic News - Monday 19th February, 1900
COLLAPSE OF NEWCASTLE – THE SOUTH FORGING AHEAD
[By Hants]

Last week I had to record that in my humble opinion Newcastle were robbed of an almost certain win by the abandonment of the Cup-tie at the Dell, but at the replay on Saturday their collapse was marked so much that it was really difficult to believe that the same teams were performing. In the course of the game Southampton scored four goals to Newcastle's one, and, besides that, put the ball into the net on five other occasions. These facts speak louder than any words I could use to convey how superior the Southern League Champions proved to be on the day's play. I would not like to say that on any occasion Southampton would be goals better than Newcastle, who, on Saturday, must have been playing streets under form. Owing to Farrell's accident last week, he was unable to play, McLeod taking his place in the centre, while Newcastle also suffered a change, Birnie taking Aitken's place at back. The latter, who played such a fine game in the abandoned match, being since down with influenza. During the week the clubs had been at cross purposes with respect to the state of the replay, but Southampton, having their regular fixture with Millwall interfered with by the cup tie between the "Dockers" and Queens Park Rangers insisted on the Saturday according to rule. It was useless for Newcastle to urge the claims of their League match with Manchester City, and in the end, after a futile appeal to the Football Association, Saturday was fixed. It was, however, not till Thursday that the ground was fit for play, and though Saturday turned out disgustingly wet the ground was playable, though slippery. Seeing how well Newcastle kept their feet on the previous frozen ground, general expectations were that a hot game would end in their favour, but this theory was soon dispelled. With an ordinary sixpenny gate the attendance was about 8000, the heavy rain keeping crowds away.

The opening stages of the game were of a startling character. Nothing much happened for some minutes, but all at once Durber missed heading a dropping shot close in front of goal, and **Peddie** finding himself absolutely alone and the ball at his feet landed it past Robinson, who could do nothing but stand still and watch the feat with a look of sad and ineffable disgust. It was a doleful start for the Saints, and seemed to preface a final ejectment from the cup, but within a minute **Turner**, with a fine cross shot, put matters as they were. It was a clever bit of work, engineered by Yates, and seemed to clean take the life out of the Newcastle men. Southampton let no grass grow under their feet, but following up the equalising goal with energy, put in some vigorous work all along the line, and **McLeod** scored a second goal. There was a strong suspicion of offside about it. MacLeod apparently having only Birnie and Kingsley in front of him when he received the ball from the rear. However the officials had no doubt on the point, and the goal, which was taken in a really clever manner by the old player, counted. This disaster still further upset the visitors, and for a considerable time we were treated to quite a puerile display on their part, of which the Saints took the fullest advantage. Their halves, prominent among whom was Chadwick, completely broke up all combination, Newcastle attacks being very rare, and though both Stephenson and W. Gardner worked very hard in the main, there was only one team in it, and so it continued up to half-time, play becoming slower as time went on.

With a lead of two to one, the game was of course a long way from being over, but after Turner had been ruled offside when he put the ball through, **McLeod** practically settled matters within 7 minutes after a very pretty little take back from Wood. Again Turner, who played with great smartness on the right, breasted through, but the point was disallowed for handling. So little signs, however, did the Newcastle men show of rallying that at this point they seemed to have lost their heads and given up hope, and it seemed any odds on Southampton winning. All at once, however, they made an unexpected brilliant combined attack which, had it been maintained, might have completely altered the result. It is also only fair to mention that Robinson, the International goalkeeper, happened to be in such form that even for him was above the average. One shot by Peddie at close range he was perhaps lucky to stop, but Fraser almost instantly sent in a grounder that Robinson secured in superb fashion. Gardiner and Stephenson, the only Newcastle pair putting any really good work on that side, made things hot for a few minutes, but a rush away ended the game to a certainty {***Yates***}. Twice after this the Saints got the ball past Kingsley, but the points did not count. Still, they were not needed, for the rout of Newcastle was utter and complete, and all interest in the game terminated long before the whistle sounded.

In reviewing the play one was struck by the fact that it was difficult to pick out a Newcastle man who put in any continuous good work. The right wing was the best, but individually Fraser on the outside left was no doubt the pick. He certainly held the upper hand of Meston, his opposing half, but it seemed to me he was not given the opportunity by his comrades that he might have had. Ghee seemed unable to hold the Saints left, Wood and Millward, two old and experienced stagers, whose knowledge of all the tricks of the game can scarcely be beaten. As Ghee was not at all well backed up by his right back, Birnie, his failure must not be altogether put down to his discredit. In fact the Newcastle backs were very weak, and this fact accounts very largely for the heavy nature of the defeat. Having said this about the losers, it now becomes an equal puzzle to throw out any of the Southampton men as failures. They were all good, and played a remarkably level game. There were times when the forwards were individually and collectively superior to the Newcastle defence. McLeod made an excellent understudy to Farrell; indeed, the latter could not have done any better. Millward and Wood I have referred to already, and their work was of a superior order. Quite in a different style was the right wing, Turner and Yates. The latter missed few chances of feeding the youngster, whose speed and excellent centring repeatedly threatened the defence of the half backs. Chadwick certainly shone. How he kept his feet, and how he anticipated the flight of the ball was surprising. He ought to be considered when Caps are being given away this season. Petrie played with even more than usual dash, but he was not quite so safe. Of the backs Durber was the cleverer as Meehan found some trouble in turning his heavy weight on the slippery ground, but was not often caught napping. Durber on several occasions covered his partner, and on the whole they did well. Robinson had little to do, but he's always a star artist. Mr. Kingscott, however, caught him napping once in taking more than two steps with the ball. As a matter of fact Robinson does this more frequently than he ought, but not every referee has the pluck to penalise him. On Saturday's form it almost seems as if choice of ground is likely to land Southampton once more in the semi-finals. At any rate that is the prevalent view at the southern seaport.

RESULT: Southampton 4 - Newcastle United 1

SOUTHAMPTON: Robinson (goal); Durber and Meehan (backs); Petrie, Chadwick and Meston (halves); Turner [1], Yates [1], McLeod [2], Wood and Milward (forwards).
NEWCASTLE UTD: Kingsley (goal); Birnie and D. Gardner (backs); Carr, Higgins and Ghee (halves); Fraser, McFarlane, Peddie [1], Stevenson and A. Gardner (forwards).
Referee: Mr. A. Kingscott (Derby)

OTHER RESULTS

27th January, 1900	Aston Villa	5–1	Bristol City
	Nottingham Forest	3–0	Sunderland
17th February, 1900	Liverpool	1–1	West Bromwich Albion
	Preston North End	1–0	Blackburn Rovers
	Sheffield United	1–1	The Wednesday
	Queens Park Rangers	0–2	Millwall Athletic
19th February, 1900	The Wednesday	0–2	Sheffield United
21st February, 1900	West Bromwich Albion	2–1	Liverpool

1899/1900 - The Third Round

Such had been the disruption caused by the weather to the Second Round of the Cup competition that when the draw was made for the Third Round on Monday 12th February, 1900, only two of the eight ties had been settled. On the original date of 27th January, three matches had been abandoned due to the heavy snows and two were abandoned prior to completion whilst one of the three played was inconclusive. The Midlands was the area least affected with the match at Birmingham (Aston Villa) and the two at Nottingham (Forest and County) being those that went ahead.

For the third time in three rounds Bury were drawn away – this time against the sharpest of the blades from the Second Round Sheffield derby, Sheffield United, the current cup holders. That Second Round derby had been a brutal and bad tempered affair, resulting in one man from each side being sent off and two Wednesday men retiring through injury, whilst several others on both sides had come out of the game badly banged about. Thus the United that faced Bury were likely to be somewhat below their best. In the infamous Willie 'Fatty' Foulke, however, they had one of the best keepers in the country, and certainly the largest.

Southern League Southampton had had the luck of a third successive home draw, in which to face their third successive First Division opponents. West Bromwich were enduring a mediocre season in League football but had a pedigree as formidable cup fighters.

SHEFFIELD UNITED v. BURY
At Bramall Lane, Shefield – Saturday 24th February, 1900
Athletic News - Monday 26th February, 1900
Among the "Roses" at Bramall Lane - County Champions in Conflict
[By Nondescript]

> Now I wish to remark, and my language is plain,
> that the way ain't so dark (nor the conflict in vain)
> for Lancashire's chance in particular,
> which the same I am free to maintain.

There is one thing about it. If the County Palatine[3] does not shortly obtain a season's lease of the Cup after many years, it can count, at any rate, one champion which has fought a good fight. I take my hat off to Bury - the best club we have for miles round this office. Financial worries and sharp-pointed luck notwithstanding, they are still in the running, and at the present time have as good a chance as any of their distinguished contemporaries. They floated the Red Rose flag in the hearts of their nearest enemies country with some show on Saturday, and if they never get any further in the struggle

---

3 Lancashire - In England, a *County Palatine* was an area ruled by a hereditary nobleman enjoying a level of autonomy separate from the rest of the kingdom. In 1351 Lancashire was made a County Palatine under Henry of Grosmont. Although these powers lapsed with Henry's Death, they were later restored and made hereditary under John of Gaunt.

they will have at least commanded admiration. Here's to 'em, then. I wouldn't think of wrecking their chances by any attempts at a forecast - for I am of a verity a false prophet. All I can recommend their naturally agitated followers is to sit tight, exercise a little more of that patience of the art of which they have shown themselves such past masters, and they may yet win the prize. They came very nearly reporting progress on Saturday, and while some who, with a club leaning maybe, think they ought to have knocked the holders out, it can truly be told that they were everywhere as good a side, and now, as they hold an "at home" their chances are ever so much brighter. Sheffield recently has seen a good deal of the Cup conflict, but an opportunity of reading another chapter in the Wars of the Roses was not to be missed, and although of course the affair did not pulse the heart of the Cutler's to such a throbbing extent as the previous meetings between the rival local factions, there was a splendid array at Bramall lane, and the upshot was a game, the like of which, so they told me, has rarely been seen there this season. The teams might, perhaps, have been more up to concert pitch. Bury were by no means certain of one or two of their players staying the proceedings out. On the other hand, the United had had to stand some battering about during the previous eight days, and they turned out to be the more unfortunate of the two, for they were unable to man the team as they would have liked, and there is no doubt about it they miss Johnson. Under the circumstances then each side could claim to have made a draw with honour.

Such games as this turned out to be are worth leaving home to see. Having been witness to a "rotter" like that at Liverpool the Saturday previous, and that bone-wearying affair at Owlerton on the Monday, it was a pleasure personally to have convincing proof that really good football - the sort which entertains, I mean - can still be played even in an English Cup tie. There was spirit in the game from the very first kick, and until the finish it was a matter of doubt which would win, the while the pace was being kept pretty hot. To begin with, Bury were very much in evidence. Their half backs for a time seem to have command of everything, and the game was only two minutes old or thereabouts when some brilliant movements on their left wing resulted in a goal, and a magnificent one, too. Plant, after putting in one ball which was not turned to account, whipped across another beauty, which was just a little too much for Foulke, and ere the big man could get within striking distance **Wood** had deftly headed past him. There were some Bury people on the ground, and they were heard from. They had some cause to be exuberant, too, for with the United team apparently taken aback and temporarily thrown out of gear fore and aft by the sudden reverse, the boys from the next county crowded on full sail, and threatened to win the match right off, Plant and Sagar giving Needham the slip and bustling up Thickett to such an extent that the cup holders and their friends were having a very bad quarter of an hour. Of course, things were bound to right themselves in time, and after Thickett had wiped some previous bad work off the slate by stopping a shot which had "goal" written on it (with Sagar's compliments), and after Morren had effected a particularly clever recovery in midfield, the United front rank showed signs of being on the premises. Almond had one hard drive, near the mark, and then an equalising goal came. For what reason the free kick was given against McLuckie I am at a loss to account. He was standing with his back to his own posts, and, reaching up, was heading the other way. Apparently he was just as much of the idea as I was, that if there was any necessity for a free kick it should have gone the other way. Boyle, however, took it, and Howard helped the ball further in, with the result that **Priest** secured as it cannoned off Pray and shot through – else Priest, of a certainty, had been offside. This turn of events naturally put new life into the United. Trickily tipping the ball over his head, then trapping it, and finally shooting for all he was worth, Priest was very near repeating his success, while Hedley was distinctly unfortunate in slipping just as he had worked to the front. But, while the United forwards were having a good deal of play, they dwelt sadly too long on the ball and were readily dispossessed, and just before the interval Bury once more took up the running. A miskick on the part of Thickett should certainly have been turned to advantage by Wood, for he had the best part of an open space to fire art. However, after Sagar had worked round three of the opposition and been finally grounded by Boyle for his pains, **McLuckie**, who had not been doing wonders up to now, fastened on a ball presented to him by Wood, who preferred not to have a pop himself, and the Bury centre, swinging half round, put his side ahead again with a shot which Foulke never had half a chance of getting to. This goal only beat the half-time whistle by a matter of seconds, …

… and seconds only had gone by, after resuming, when Bury ought to have been leading three goals to one. To be exact, Hedley had a reasonable chance, instanter, of doing his side some good, Priest placing well to him, only to see him aim wide. But Wood could almost have scored with his eyes shut, for Plant had enticed Foulke away from his keep, and as the ball came across the delinquent had an unprotected goal to simply walk through. Instead he slipped and missed fire altogether. After these ceremonies the United once again bucked up, and Thomson having his fill of good shots, had at last to face the ordeal of a penalty. Case for the plaintiffs was one of handling against Darroch, and **Needham** made no mistake when entrusted with the customary punishment - two up in the little man's favour within the week. The game was very nearly being won and lost on several occasions before the finish. Whereon, however, the United bunched up in front of goal and looked like sweeping the decks, particularly when Thomson was penalised for carrying the ball, Bury were the oftener threatening danger, scurries on their wings which frequently beat the backs, and one surprise package which they gave Foulke before the end deserves mention. The visitors had been given a free kick, and Pray, instead of going on with it in the usual way, tapped the ball to Darroch. The back looked like making ample atonement for his costly mistake earlier on. He had nearly a fifty yards shot, and Foulke, prepared for nothing of this kind, saw the ball come swishing in at the far corner of the goal at a forty-mile-per-hour pace. The keeper looked beaten all the way, and only a giant could have saved the situation. Save it however, Foulke did. It was just a case of getting one fist there, and the "thwack" of the colliding ball told of the power behind it. For a long range shot it was about the best I have ever seen.

Well, the Bury boys are bonnie boys. They deserved all they got, and they had the heartiest reception on leaving the ground, for right now there were some thousands of Wednesday sympathisers round the playing pitch, and the visitors all along suffered nothing for want of encouragement. I believe, however, they would have played pretty much the same game had they not had a single shouter, for in addition to being a rare plucked lot they are just built for the job. They were, of course, never fighting an up-hill battle like their opponents', and an early goal means a lot in a Cup tie, but the credit attaching to their performance is undeniable. At the same time it must not be forgotten that the United were handicapped missing a man like Johnson, who is good enough to wear an international cap any day. His absence had the effect, in my mind, that the intermediate line was not so straight backed as usual, for though Howard must really be given credit as being a useful chap, sturdy, and obstructive, one does not need telling which of the two would be played, both fit and well. Rightly divining which was the most dangerous wing, Needham set himself to look after Sagar and Plant, and sometimes did so well, and sometimes not so, for Sagar, who took the eye as the cleverest forward on the field, despite some hard knocks which he received, very frequently drew the International on, and then adroitly placed the ball to where Plant had a clear course. And some of the movement's executed by the Bury left wing took rank among the titbits of the afternoon. Richards and Wood, however, if not so clever or so dangerous made excellent progress, and it struck me that McLuckie could have held his wings better on occasions. As it was, the Bury forwards had the most chances of winning the match, and they ought to have done so, for they had the weakest pair of backs to operate against, while Foulke was no worthier a foe to face than Thomson. McLuckie was indirectly the cause of both United's goals. As stated, he was adjudged to have committed a foul - no foul at all in my estimation - which paved the way to the first point, and then he was hopping about and trying to show off a few tricks that were quite useless on such going and against such a Jack-in-the-box as Morren, with the result that the ball was instantly banged to the other end of the field, where Darroch conceded a penalty. But the goal he took himself was a very fine effort. As on previous occasions, the Bury half-back line was a solid affair, and though Ross did seem to be somewhat "blown" towards the end, he stood up with grim tenacity. An English Cup medal after thirteen years' service is a nice bauble to dream about, George, and we have seen a worse team than Bury carry the prize off. They looked winners right enough at one time in the second half on Saturday, so stubbornly did their backs meet every attack, and that expensive affair of handling by Darroch was the only fault which marred a magnificent show of defence. There was little in it on the whole, though the United might be accounted somewhat lucky in drawing level. Considering the gruelling they have had lately, and the fact that they met their opponents at a disadvantage in point of strength, they did well, however, and methinks they are likely to do just as creditably on Thursday. I have seen their forwards to much better advantage. Too often they were pirouetting and working too much on the circular tour ticket, with the result that they were charged excess fares, so to speak. Priest, though, deserves mention, for he was the oftener doing the right thing. The visitors front line were smarter on the ball, and as a rule found the nearest way to the goal, fearing not Foulke even when he loomed up big on the landscape. Just as I liked Sagar in the Bury team, so did I have a good deal of regard for Beers on the opposing attack. Both players catch the eye at once, and combine a cleverness when in command of the ball with discretion in placing it. Outside wingers can scarcely help making ground with such partners, and I should like to see them one on either side of G.O. Smith. They'd make their partners gallop, also the opposition. With Needham not always happy, Morren took the honours as a consistent half-back, and I do think the little chap would be some use against those Scotch forwards. It would be like slipping a spring heeled Jack amongst them. We shall be very badly off for backs, however, if Thickett gets his cap again. It was well for the party in stripes that Boyle was sure footed, and he was banging away with a straight left when everything else was beaten. Poor Peter has been put through the mill lately for doing things which such a fine old Irish gentleman ought to be ashamed of. He kept his hands off the "dirrty worruk" on Saturday; was, in fact, an injured innocent, for once Wood tried to vault on his breastbone, while on another occasion Pray rattled his ankles quite as lustily as they tickle the pates at Donnybrook[4]. But Peter did nothing more than assume a countenance which said "Another injustice to Ireland" more eloquently than words.

> And so the next call is to Bury, me boys, on Thursday.
> And if, after all is done, and whether or not the cup be won,
> I hear any more complaints of chronic impecuniosity at Gigg lane,
> may I smight the Secretary for a tale-pitcher.

RESULT: Sheffield United 2 – Bury 2

BURY: Thompson (goal); Darroch and Davidson (backs); Pray, Leeming and Ross (halves); Richards, Wood [1], McLuckie [1], Sagar and Plant (forwards).
SHEFFIELD UTD: Foulke (goal); Thickett and Boyle (backs); Needham [1^{pen}], Morren and Howard (halves); Bennett, Beers, Hedley, Almond and Priest [1] (forwards).
Referee: Mr. A. Kingscott (Derby)

The event of the replay at Gigg Lane coincided with a day of national celebration following the relief of Ladysmith[5]. This was especially celebrated in Lancashire due to the heroic actions of the 11th Lancashire Brigade in the relief column, who fought through several levels of determined resistance to reach the besieged town, then repulsed several ferocious counter-attacks before overwhelming the enemy ranged against them and putting them to flight in great disarray. Consequently, in an outpouring of local and national pride, many Lancashire mills and factories shut down for the day, giving their employees a day's holiday. Spontaneous celebrations took place in several towns and cities across Lancashire, with flag waving citizens packing into the main public places – an estimated 7,000 gathering in the market square at Lancaster alone. Others headed for the one football match taking place in the County Palatine on that day, enormously swelling the crowd at Gigg Lane. Consequently, there was chaos at Manchester's Victoria station where fans flooded in from all parts of Lancashire as well as those bearing the red and white favours of the visitors from Yorkshire – packing aboard every train destined for Bury until the carriages could bear no more. In Bury itself, long before kick-off time the approaches to the ground were thronged with a constant stream of would-be spectators, many waving Union Jack's and in many cases being packed so tightly together that it was impossible to do other than travel along with the majority. The number of paying patrons, later estimated at around 25,000, set a new record for the ground, but since an estimated 3,000 more forced their way in without paying after officials tried to close the gates to an already packed ground against them the actual number was probably in excess of 28,000. Under the circumstances it was greatly feared that playing the match to a finish would prove impossible, but the good nature and exemplary behaviour of the crowd kept encroachment to a minimum, allowing the match to proceed without incident.

---

4 Town in Ireland (now Republic of), once famous for vicious drunken brawls in connection with it's annual fair. Became a byword for violent disorder. Tickle the pates = strike on the heads.
5 A garrison city in the Kwazulu-Natal region of South Africa, which had been surrounded and cut-off for four months by enemy forces in the 2nd Boer War.

BURY v. SHEFFIELD UNITED (Replay)
At Gigg Lane, Bury – Thursday 1st March, 1900
Manchester Courier - Friday 2nd March, 1900

At Bury, before 22,000 spectators. Bury played their strongest team, and Johnson reappeared in the United team. Pray won the toss, and set United to face the wind.

Bury immediately got away, but Thickett returned, and Darroch checked Priest and Almond. A sudden rush by McLuckie and Richards was only saved at the last moment by Foulke dashing out and kicking away. Thompson was called upon by Almond, and then Bury pressed, and the goal had a marvellous escape from centres by Richards and Wood, and Foulke saved from McLuckie. Bury exercised a good deal of pressure, and several times Foulke had to clear from dangerous attacks. Two corners were dangerous, and then from a free kick Richards headed in, Plant missing just at the post. Again Bury ran up and Plant was going for the goal when Foulke and Thickett, getting the worst of the encounter, play was stopped for minute. Bury kept hovering round the goal, but the United's defence was fine. Bury continued to apply the pressure, and it was really wonderful how the goal escaped downfall. Four more corners fell to Bury, and all were splendidly put in, but the backs and custodian were in their liveliest form and kept the forwards out. Shots by Plant, Sagar, McLuckie, and Davidson were cleverly cleared by Foulke, who was in tip-top form. Thickett twisted his knee and was carried off. Priest missed with an open goal. Interval: Bury, nil; United, nil.

On resuming. Thickett made a re-appearance, but although United now had the wind Bury kept them on the defensive, and had won two corners in as many minutes. The United rarely got down, and Thompson had practically nothing to do. Several times Bury were swarming round the United's goal, but each time the defenders were too much on the alert. Needham was hurt, but he resumed, and play continued well in Bury's favour, the United only getting down occasionally, and then giving practically very little trouble. Thompson cleared, and then the Bury men went away right merrily, and **Richards** securing, he banged through 27 minutes after the restart. The crowd cheered vociferously for several minutes. At this stage Needham left the ground limping, and did not return. Roused by this reverse, the United made a big effort to get on terms, but the defence was really fine, end they were quickly driven back. At the end of 40 minutes Richards secured and gave **Plant** a lovely pass, and that player, who was close to the post, headed past Foulke in a twinkling, and again the crowd cheered. A free kick for a foul was awarded the United, but the danger was averted. Another stiff attack was commenced on the United's goal, and Sagar sent in a stinging shot at close quarters, which Foulke was lucky to tip over the bar. Several attempts were made at the goal, but without anything tangible accruing.

RESULT: Bury 2 - Sheffield Utd 0

BURY: Thompson (goal); Darroch and Davidson (backs); Pray, Leeming and Ross (halves); Richards [1], Wood, McLuckie, Sagar and Plant [1] (forwards).
SHEFFIELD UTD: Foulke (goal); Thickett and Boyle (backs); Needham, Morren and Howard (halves); Bennett, Beers, Hedley, Almond and Priest (forwards).

Referee: Mr. A. Kingscott (Derby)

After the match, enthusiasm over the home club's victory added to the general enthusiasm of the day led to scenes in the town not unlike those commonly following a victory in the Cup Final itself – a portent, perhaps, of events yet to come!

SOUTHAMPTON v. WEST BROMWICH ALBION
At The Dell, Southampton – Saturday 24th February, 1900
Athletic News - Monday 26th February, 1900
West Bromwich Albion Ousted - The Southern Sun Still Shining
[By Hants]

Southampton's victory over the Albion at Southampton on Saturday, landing the Southerners into the semi-final for the second time was thoroughly deserved. During the course of as bad a nineteen minutes play as the biggest glutton for football might ever hope to see, they had considerably the best of the game, and their triumph by 2 to 1, not inaptly perhaps, represented the ebb and flow of the play. It should, of course, not be overlooked that in defeating such stubborn opponents in succession as Everton, Newcastle, and West Bromwich, the "Saints" had on each occasion the estimable advantage of choice of ground. Only a few years back that would have been considered a fair handicap for a League team going south, but the team that has won the Southern League thrice in succession, is in its composition as near a facsimile of any Northern professional club as could be imagined, and one need only glance at the names of the players on both sides to be struck by the fact that, in point of the employment of experienced players, the Southern team had, if anything, the advantage. Up to now the South has produced few first class men, and, with one exception the winning team on Saturday was composed of ex-players of League clubs. Several of them like Wood, Milward, and McLeod for instance, had been dropped from their old clubs, and yet seemed to retain all the fire and vigour of youth, or to have marvellously renewed it. At the same time one could not help feeling it to be a pity that a team like the Albion, that had struggled so gamely through two rounds, and around whose heads was the Glory of having five times been in a Final tie, and twice winners of the Cup, should be ejected at the present stage. We are getting accustomed to rain or snow every Saturday now, but it certainly was very depressing at the Dell. The ground was soaked to such an extent that a walking stick pushed with moderate force would sink in 3 inches almost anywhere. Still the surface was in wonderful condition considering all things, and seemed to trouble the players very little. The attendance was not large, about 8,000 in all, but it contained several high and mighty personages, not forgetting Mornington Cannon[6], who is gone on[7] the Southampton club. I was surprised to see Mr. R.P. Gregson, wandered all the way from Blackburn, in the enclosure, likewise Mr. C.J. Hughes, of Cheshire, and when I also saw Mr. G.S. Sherington, of London, I looked round for the ponderous form of Mr. Percy Timbs, but he was missing at the start. However, he turned up at half-time, having been delayed in town by being empanelled on a Grand Jury which, on Saturday, to an enthusiast like

---

6 a.k.a. 'Morny Cannon,' champion jockey and British Triple Crown winner (1899), born near Southampton at Houghton.
7 'gone on' (archaic) – taken by, attracted to, has affection for.

him, was a source of great disgust. With such eyes on the match the credit of the south was at stake, and, as a Southerner, I am glad the "Saints" won, but it wanted a lot of winning. At first the "Saints" displayed cleverer football, and had some very hard luck. Half an hour's play saw the "Throstles" ahead, and yet up to half-time how their goal escaped was astonishing so hardly were they pressed. Then in the second half the "Saints" seemed to get their tails down, and to be completely disorganised. Meantime, the Albion, bold in their opponents' extremity, played a hard slogging game that looked likely to increase their lead. Then came the equalising goal, and after that a complete turn of the tables, and a final win in spite of some rough and heavy play on the part of the visitors in their last desperate struggles. It was Cup-tie football, pure and simple, and not a creditable display by the beaten side. The teams lined up in driving rain that never once stopped.

The "Saints" went off vigorously, and for some minutes seemed all over their opponents, Reader being busy too often to be enjoyable. The Albion, slower in getting moving, then took up the running, and several free kicks for minor offences, dangerously threatened the home goal. In their eagerness both Perry and Simmons were penalised for charging Robinson, and I was glad to see the referee straight on this dangerous practice. Milward had a stroke of bad luck, as he was given offside when he had cleverly beaten Adams, and put the ball past Reader. It was a very close thing, but Mr. Bye was near at the time, and had a good view. Still it had a bad effect on the "Saints," and for a time they lost ground, resulting in **Simmons** beating Robinson with a cross shot yards out of his reach. This was a facer for the locals, but they never lost heart, and indeed attacked brilliantly, the Albion goal having some narrow escapes. Reader saved superbly, and the backs were very firm, Adams, if anything, being smarter than Williams. The Albion scored again, but an infraction of the holding regulation rendered the point useless, and so came half-time with the team that had done least work leading by a goal.

On restarting, the "Saints" had every appearance of a beaten side, and seemed all at sea. Robinson was there, of course, and was the only one to put on a bold front. West Bromwich played a hard slogging game, every man going in with both feet, but there was nothing brilliant about it, though enough to utterly upset the "Saints," who only seldom were dangerous. The turning point came at last, but it was rather an unusual one. Reader was well behind his goal line when he saved, and saved magnificently, a grounder from **Wood**, and the referee held a consultation with his linesmen. When he pointed to the centre didn't the good old welkin bell ring. Still, it was a bit of hard luck, and that foot, if it was so much behind the line, spelt defeat. For the remainder of the play things were a bit rough, particularly on the Albion's part, but in the main the "Saints" pressed, and five minutes from time **McLeod** drove a back pass from Wood into goal, and so won the match. I may be considered to have some leaning in favour of the "Saints," but hope not; yet I am bound to say that in this match as in those against Everton and Newcastle, the winners played cleverer football. On neither of these occasions have Southampton people been shown any new combination of superior tactics, and in spite of some provocation the winners abstained from degenerating into mere roughness. Even in the half hour in the second part, when the Albion looked to have the result in hand, their combination was not equal to that of their opponents. The right wing played one style and the left another, Chadburn treating the onlookers to a series of single handed runs, while Roberts and Richards stuck to close passing. The feature of the Albion was their defence. Reader did not suffer even in comparison with Robinson, though he had more to do, but the energy and determination of the halves and backs formed perhaps the stiffest defensive play there has been seen at Southampton for some years. Adams showed great ability and accuracy, and was rarely passed, and, for so youthful looking a player, he came to a high standard. Williams was, of course, the cynosure of all eyes, and his only fault, and that rather apparent, was his slowness both in turning and running. As the local spectators are used to Peter Meehan's huge kicks, the International's powerful returns created no surprise. He was beaten rather too often for so renowned a back. All the halves were sound, obstinate, and spirited. Jones, apart from his curious method of heading the ball, was the best, but Hadley, who was unwearied, quite telescoped the Turner-Yates combination, and when that goes the "Saints" are at a disadvantage. Dunn, with his tattooed arms bare to the elbows, played vigorously, and checked Milward too often to be pleasant to that player. Of the forwards Simmons was the best, passing unselfishly and leading the defence a long and stern chase. Perry's judicious placing of the ball was quite a noticeable feature, and there were many occasions on which Roberts and Richardson nonplussed Sammy Meston, but the strength of them lay in the defence. The team seemed well balanced, and with no especially shining light. In contrast to Williams and Adams the Southampton backs suffered, and I incline to the belief that the untiring work of the halves was more responsible for the win than anything else. Chadwick was here, there, and everywhere, and shone both in attack and defence, and the trio once again showed the great value of a fast, tricky, and obstinate set of halves. McLeod in the absence of Farrell, injured a fortnight ago, again distinguished himself, and it is difficult to see how he can be dropped. Turner seemed a bit overawed by Williams, but several times tricked him cleverly. Yates devotion to his young partner is marked, and does him credit. Harry Wood played a surprisingly fresh game, full of resource, and also received some heavy attentions from Jones and Dunn, once being carried off the field and unconscious for some minutes. Football begins to tell on the old stager, worse luck. Milward was not so successful as usual, finding Adams quite as sharp as himself. It was not a great game, but one well worth watching and the better side on the whole won.

RESULT: Southampton 2 – West Bromwich Albion 1

SOUTHAMPTON: Robinson (goal); Durber and Meehan (backs); Petrie, Chadwick and Meston (halves); Turner, Yates, McLeod [1], Wood [1] and Milward (forwards).
WEST BROMWICH: Reader (goal); Williams and Adams (backs); Hadley, Jones and Dunn (halves); Roberts, Richards, Simmons [1], T. Perry and Chadburn (forwards).
Referee: Mr. F. Bye (Sheffield)

After the match, the greatest indignation prevailed in the Midlands regarding the alleged mistakes perpetrated by match referee Mr. Bye which had, in their view, cost the Albionites the game. These were:
1) *That the supposed infraction connected with Albion's disallowed 'goal' just before the interval was non-existent.*
2) *That goalkeeper Reader's foot was in front of the line, not behind it, when he kicked away Wood's shot so that the ball did not in fact enter the goal.*

3) That Southampton's Jones should have been dismissed for the illegal challenge on Wood that caused the latter to miss several minutes of the game.

With regard to the latter, Mr. J.S. Sherrington, a member of the F.A. disciplinary committee who was present at the match, had asked the referee after the final whistle, in the presence of Frank Heaven, secretary of the Albion club, why he did not dismiss Jones following the challenge, Mr. Bye replying that in his opinion Jones could not help himself due to the treacherous state of the ground. Regardless of the referee's explanation, Mr. Sherrington reported the player to the investigative committee, but no subsequent action was taken against club or player.

OTHER RESULTS

24th February, 1900   Millwall Athletic   1–1   Aston Villa
                               Preston North End   0–0   Nottingham Forest

28th February, 1900   Nottingham Forest   1–0   Preston North End

5th March, 1900   Millwall Athletic   2–1   Aston Villa

1899/1900 - Semi-Finals

The vagaries of the draw for the Semi-Finals ensured that both ties would be of special interest. In the first, Bury, having already knocked one of the two Notts. clubs out of the competition were now drawn against the other in an all First Division affair, whilst in the second the two remaining Southern League clubs were pitted together, thus ensuring a representative of that League in the Final for the first time ever.

Of the four remaining clubs, only Nottingham Forest had any significant pedigree in the competition, having reached the Semi-Final stage three times previously and lifted the trophy once in 22 years continual involvement in the competition. Southampton had reached the Semi-Final stage once previously, two years earlier, on which occasion they had been knocked out by the Foresters. For both Bury and Millwall, on the other hand, reaching this stage of the competition was breaking new ground.

As well as enjoying the best historical records in the current competition, Forest and Southampton each rode higher in their respective Leagues than their Semi-Final opponents. Bury, however, had reached this stage the hard way, drawn away in every round and always against First League opposition, whilst Millwall had knocked out three times winners Aston Villa in the 3rd Round on their own route to this stage. Consequently, if the first pair were the favourites it was only by a tiny margin.

Bury seemed likely to be without their influential captain, Pray, who in the days before the match had been suffering from an attack of muscular rheumatism in his left leg – a condition that restricted movement and caused him acute pain. Forest, on the other hand, were certain to be absent the services of England right-half Frank Forman, who was down with pneumonia, his brother Fred also being doubtful. The neutral venue, at Stoke, if anything conveyed more advantage to the Buryites, but only because of the Foresters poor away record, having not gained a single victory outside of the lace city that season - their only 'away' success having come in a League encounter against city neighbours Notts. County.

The choice of Crystal Palace for the Millwall v. Southampton game, meanwhile, was somewhat controversial since some felt it took away from the 'specialness' of reserving that venue for the final!

BURY v. NOTTINGHAM FOREST
at the Victoria Ground, Stoke - Saturday 24th March, 1900
Athletic News - Monday 26th March, 1900
A Poor Game at Stoke - Bury and Nottingham Forest Draw
[By the Free Critic]

When Bury and Nottingham Forest were discovered together in the semi-final for the English cup it was felt that there were only two really convenient grounds - at Stoke and Sheffield. Birmingham was mentioned, and certainly no more commodious enclosure than that at Aston could be desired, but it is a long way from Bury, and, on the whole, Stoke was the most desirable centre. It is not the first semi-final that has been played in the potteries, for didn't Derby Junction meet West Bromwich Albion there after so unexpectedly disposing of the favourites Blackburn Rovers? Then the Albion and the Rovers also played at Stoke, and three years ago Everton and Derby County met. On this occasion 33,000 people put in an appearance and then, as now, the arrangements were in the hands of Mr. W. Heath. Their excellence had probably a great deal to do with the Bury and Nottingham Forest match being played in the potteries, and all week Mr. Heath and the officials of the Stoke club have been busy making everything perfect. The railway companies did their best, and all round the match has had a capital advertisement. For once in a way, Bury folks thought they would distinguish themselves, and promptly engaged a train and saloons. I don't know whether they had to pay the ridiculous charge of £1 which the railway people have decided to charge for each saloon. Burslem Port Vale did not view the Cup-tie with the most pleasant feelings, and it was distinctly hard lines on them to have to forgo one of the best gates of the season, for the Bolton Wanderers are a good draw to second division clubs. However, had they played, the ground at Corbridge would have presented a deserted appearance, for the populace of the potteries literally emptied itself into Stoke on Saturday afternoon. Opinions as well as sympathy, were equally divided between the two teams, and in that particular, not a more neutral spot could have been selected. As is well known, Bury appeared in the semi-final for the first time, but the Forest have been there before, and reached that stage in 1879, when Oxford University threw them out. I think the Forest team of that year was one of the best I ever saw. Perhaps as they threw my old club out by six goals to none I have an exaggerated idea of their prowess, but up to meeting the Forest - in December - we had not been beaten. They had a peculiar formation, and I will give the way Sam Widowson disposed of his men:

```
                        Sands
                        Cabora
            E. Luntley          W. Luntley
              Biggs               Ackroyd
   Goodyer            Smith              Widowson
              Turner              Earp
```

We had a wholesome respect for the Reds I can tell you. By the way, this was the first time I ever saw leg-guards, Sam Widowson wore them. One could go on for a long time writing about ancient football, but we had better proceed to the semi-final at Stoke. The weather was not what you'd consider genial, but, for football, it was as good as you could wish. There was a sample of Boreas[8], but it was an uncertain quantity - that is to say we never knew which direction he was blowing, so that when Pray lost the toss he did not go much astray. The crowd was not of the dimensions anticipated, and 20,000 would be a liberal estimate, the receipts amounting to £768. The shilling side, nearest to the town, was not crowded, but the sixpenny people turned up alright, and occupied all available space. We were, however, decidedly comfortable, and I did not hear anyone grumble. Free Staters[9] from Bury and Nottingham were very much in evidence, and the Notts. people brought with them flags of red, but the Bury white one was conspicuous by its absence. The coffee tent caterer had "success to the winning team" emblazoned on his emporium, but he also displayed a red and a white flag, so that his neutrality should not be mistaken. The Foresters arrived in the potteries on Friday from Skegness, and put up at the new Grand Hotel at Hanley. Bury, who find the Gigg-lane breeze is quite sufficient, left the Lancashire town at 12 o'clock noon, and seemed to be fit as possible. It was generally thought that the captain, Pray, would be unable to play, but he duly turned out. On the other hand, the Forest were without the brothers Foreman, and in the case of Frank, they were decidedly unfortunate, for the international half-back is just the man to break up the Bury combination.

There was no great advantage in winning the toss, for the wind did not seem to know its own mind. Bury had the best of the opening exchanges, but the first quarter of an hour was absolutely the tamest display of football I have ever witnessed between two first-class teams. Bury scored first from a penalty {***Pray***, *13 mins*}. It is seldom we see penalty kicks awarded in either the semi-final or final tie, but there was no doubt about the one on Saturday, for Ironmonger made no mistake in fisting the ball from under the bar. I don't like penalty kicks, but in this case it was fully justified, and not only so, but the assault which caused Ironmonger to take the goalkeepers place *pro tem*, was well worth a goal - in fact, it was the best and most solid attack of the afternoon. The Forest goal came from a free kick within the 12 yards line, and the ball was put clean across to **Capes**, who headed it past Thomson. This represented the scoring, and an enthusiastic Forest friend of mine almost knocked my shoulder out of joint in emphasizing his opinion that there would be no further scoring. He turned out to be quite correct, and there were few occasions indeed after the interval where either side seemed likely to score. Bury had more chances, but failed to utilise them, and in the last 5 minutes the Forest were probably more dangerous than at any previous period of the game. Both sides appeared afraid less something should happen, and played the kicking out game to perfection. No one seemed particularly sorry when Mr. Scragg blew his whistle, with the result a draw of one reach. I have seen a good many semi-finals during the last 20 years, but, without being too severe, I should say Saturday's was the worst. There was scarcely a sparkling moment. I did not expect much of a scientific order from Bury but certainly hoped for something of the sort from the Forest. Well, what pretty football we saw was on the Bury side, and that wasn't much to boast about. We had little enthusiasm, but there was quite as much as the occasion demanded, for, to tell the truth, there was little to enthuse about. Had we not known from the correct list of players that the teams were representative, we should have been fully justified in thinking that they were reserve elevens. In Cup ties you don't expect to see the best of football, but you do expect something much different to what we had at Stoke on

---

8   Boreas – Greek God of the wind.
9   Free Staters – [archaic] Those aligned to a particular cause.

Saturday. The only really good man on the Forest side was McPherson, and he was the oldest of the crew. He played a genuine game, and was not only full of energy, but displayed rare judgment. So far as the others were concerned there was not a bright spot in them if I except some strong kicking, and also tackling on the part of Peers, who was a capital back. I have seen better, but Peers is quite clever enough for ordinary purposes, McPherson was, however, the shining light. There is a semblance of staleness in his movements, as might be expected, but he was always knock-everyone[10], for I never saw such a lackadaisical lot. I suppose they had an idea that they were fighting for a place at the Crystal Palace on April 21, but to the ordinary observer they seem to be playing one of the "friendlies" we hear so much of. To make a draw suggests all sorts of things, but I am perfectly convinced that it was a keen trial of strength, and that either side would have given a bit to appear in the final. Allsop had more to do than Thomson, but that wasn't saying much, for it is seldom two goalkeepers in such an important match have the less work. Even then Ironmonger considered that Allsop required assistance, but his efforts were not attended with great success, for the consequent penalty meant Bury's only goal. The Lancashire men had the better opportunities of scoring, and what Sagar was thinking about just before half time I cannot conceive. He had the goal at his mercy on the 12 yards mark, with no one in front of him, but he shot wildly wide. I hope Spencer shapes better at Cardiff this afternoon, for certainly he didn't show anything approaching international form on Saturday, and it was not because he was poorly fed, for Morris happened to be about the best forward of the lot, and put in good, honest work. But all round, the forward display was poor in the extreme, and decidedly disappointing to those who knew what the Forest front rank is capable of. Possibly Fred Foreman may have improved them, but the man they missed most was brother Frank, although Coles did not do badly for a first appearance in such an important match. The Bury defence was not so sound as we generally find it. Darroch is usually as safe as a rock, but on Saturday he kicked blindly, and tackled badly. Thompson had not much to do and could not be blamed for the shot which beat him, although it seemed such a simple one. Davidson was much in front of Darroch, but I've seen him better. Bury were strong at half-back, and it was chiefly owing to the persistent efforts of Pray, Leeming, and Ross that the ball was kept so much in the Reds Territory. They formed a hard-working trio, and gave their forwards every chance, but the latter left each other to their own, when following up would have paid much better. Wood was perhaps the more serviceable of the five, for McLuckie was too well looked after by McPherson to be very dangerous. Richards ran gamely, and Sagar put in some nice touches, but often passed the ball too hard for Plant to take it along. The outside left made some lively lovely centres, and was always dangerous when in close quarters. I am looking forward to a much better exposition of the game when the teams meet on Thursday at Bramall-lane. There is one thing about it, they cannot play worse than on Saturday.

RESULT: Bury 1 – Nottingham Forest 1

BURY: Thompson (goal); Darroch and Davidson (backs); Pray [1^{pen}], Leeming and Ross (halves); Richards, Wood, McLuckie, Sagar and Plant (forwards).

---

10 Knock-everyone – [archaic] the best / knocking the rest out of contention.

NOTTINGHAM FOREST: Allsop (goal); Ironmonger and Peers (backs); Norris, McPherson ans Coles (halves); Spouncer, Morris, Beveridge, Calvey and Capes [1] (forwards).
Referee: Mr. A. Scragg (Crewe)

BURY v. NOTTINGHAM FOREST (Replay)
at Bramall Lane, Sheffield - Thursday 29th March, 1900
Manchester Courier - Friday 30 March 1900
Replayed Semi-Final Tie – A Memorable Game
Sensational Success of the Lancashire Club

After the drawn game at Stoke these well-known clubs met at Bramall-lane, Sheffield, yesterday afternoon, to decide which organisation should meet Southampton in the Final. The extraordinary number of drawn games in the Cup competition this season has extended interest to a large degree, and certain it is that not for many years, has the tourney proved so exciting. Each club has an excellent record and although Forest have a slight advantage, as far as their respective positions in the League go, the teams are very well-matched as witness last Saturday's encounter at Stoke. In the League meetings Bury have shown themselves slightly the better team, making a draw (2 goals each) at Nottingham and winning at home by two goals to one. What the clubs have done in the Cup-ties will be gleaned from the following:

BURY: First round - beat Burnley, at Burnley (1-0); Second round - beat Notts County, at Bury (2-0), after draw at Nottingham (0-0); Third round - beat Sheffield United (holders), at Bury (2-0), after draw at Sheffield (2-2); Semi-final - drew with Notts Forest, Stoke (1-1).
NOTTINGHAM FOREST: First round - beat Grimsby Town, at Nottingham (3-0); Second round - beat Sunderland, at Nottingham (3-0); Third round - beat Preston North End, Nottingham (1-0), after draw at Preston (0-0); Semi-final - drew with Bury at Stoke (1-1).

It will thus be seen that Forest have the better goal average, viz., eight goals to one, against Bury eight to three, but seeing that the Lancashire team were drawn away each time, the latter's performance in reaching the semi-final was the better one. Bury were relying on the same team which has done well this season, and as usual, the players had undergone their training operations at home. Notts. Forest had hoped to enjoy the services of Fred Forman, forward, but he, like his brother Frank, was unable to play, and thus the team that took the field yesterday was exactly the same as played on Saturday. Luckily, the weather was fairly favourable, with entire absence of any wind, but the turf had been rendered very greasy on the top, and something like a fog threatened. The light, however, very misty at the start, improved somewhat as the game was in progress. A big crowd assembled to witness the encounter, the gate being officially returned at 11,200, and the gate receipts at £445. Half-past three was the hour fixed upon for the kick-off, but shortly before that time the news travelled round that the Bury men had not arrived, and the start was consequently postponed. Soon afterwards, however, the Forest team entered the enclosure, and were followed after an interval by the Bury players, the commencement of the match being delayed for nearly a quarter of an hour.

Having had to hurry on to the field, Bury were naturally not at their ease, and far from settling down they were all at sea for the first few minutes. The Forest smartly took advantage of the handicap under which their opponents laboured, and before the game had been in progress much more than a couple of minutes, looked to have won the game. Less than a minute had elapsed after McLuckie had kicked off than Spouncer raced down, and finishing with a good centre, **Capes** dashed the ball into the net, thus scoring the first goal for the Forest. Almost directly following the re-start the Forest had a free-kick awarded them, and Thompson, in saving, nearly put through his own goal. For the moment he, cleared, but that was all, for **Calvey** got on the ball and sent it between the posts, the Nottingham club being two goals up almost before the game had commenced. The Forest were playing much better football than their opponents, and Thompson saved from Beveridge. He was fouled in doing so, and Ross and Sagar worked the ball down, only to see Plant shoot yards wide. Then Morris and Spouncer again worked down, but Darroch cleared at close quarters. Still Notts attacked strongly, Bury being quite demoralised. A couple of fouls, one to either side, resulted in nothing, and then Sagar, after a fine dribble, was dispossessed by Peers, who kicked wildly into touch. Even play followed, but the Bury passing was wild and ill-timed, and Peers and Iremonger easily dealt with the somewhat weak attack. At length Sagar and Plant combined capitally, and a magnificent centre from the last-named was admirably cleared by Iremonger. Then Capes forced a corner off Davidson, but brilliant play by Darroch enabled the Lancashire team to press, and Plant almost scored with a grand screw shot, which Allsop cleared grandly and Forest got down, but Capes was given off-side. Further brilliant play by Plant, following good work by Ross, enabled Bury to gain the first corner. This proved abortive, and the Notts forwards, who were very quick on the ball, attacked, and Thompson saved brilliantly from Calvey. Mid-field play ensued, and after Peers had effected a grand clearance, Forest again attacked but found Thompson in his best form. The Bury right wing at length got a chance, and Richards, with his usual dash, centred but the defence prevailed, and though Iremonger cleared, Bury were soon attacking, and McLuckie headed over the bar. Sagar next shot wide, and Forest were hard pressed. Ultimately a weak pass by Plant enabled Peers to relieve, but the Lancashire men again returned to the attack, and McLuckie was pulled up with a clear course. Plant, who was in great form, initiated a hot attack on the Forest goal, and Allsop saved a grand shot from Wood after superb passing. A long shot from Peers next went over the bar. Half-time score: Notts Forest, 2 goals; Bury, nil.

For the first few minutes after change of ends the Forest players distinctly held the upper hand, and Thompson made a magnificent save from Capes, who had a clear course, but the Bury goalkeeper took the ball from his toes. Thompson also saved from Calvey, and a few minutes later he made a wonderful save from Spouncer. Allsop next at the other end saved from Sagar, two abortive corners following. The Forest defenders were not very particular in their methods, and they were several times penalised for fouls, one glaring instance being when Peers brought McLuckie down near the 12 yards line. The "Shakers," however, appeared to be a beaten team, their efforts lacking method, and though they struggled pluckily all hopes of appearing at the Crystal Palace had disappeared. **Sagar**, however, altered the prospect by scoring, this success taking place twenty minutes from what would ordinarily have been the finish. Thus encouraged Bury got to work in most determined style, and their success seemed to somewhat upset the Notts. backs, who more than once kicked faultily. In the last quarter of an hour Bury had all the play, the Forest goal being subjected to continual bombardment, and the Notts. backs repeatedly kicked out. Three corners followed in quick succession, and it was wonderful how the Forest goal escaped. The ball was continually near the Notts. citadel, but try as they would Bury could not score till the last minute, when they equalised from a corner, **McLuckie** heading into the net, thus making the score two goals each.

An extra half hour had thus to be played, and Bury played with great dash. Nothing came of their attacks, however, whereas from a pass by Beveridge, Morris sent in a fine shot, the ball hitting Thompson's knee and rebounding into play. This was a lucky escape for Bury, who held their own, but that was all, to the close of the first extra fifteen minutes. A fine match then looked like coming to a tame conclusion for the Notts men were somewhat exhausted, and the Bury players seemed in a similar plight. However, the Lancashire lads had something left, and during the concluding stages of the contest they completely outplayed the Forest. McLuckie narrowly missed giving his side the lead, but this honour fell to **Sagar**, who, with little more than five minutes left, gave Bury their third goal. Before the end came the Forest attacked once or twice, and Thompson had to handle, but when the end came Bury could claim a gallant victory.

RESULT: Bury 3 – Nottingham Forest 2 (aet)

BURY: Thompson (goal); Darroch and Davidson (backs); Pray, Leeming and Ross (halves); Richards, Wood, McLuckie [1], Sagar [2] and Plant (forwards).
NOTTINGHAM FOREST: Allsop (goal); Peers and Iremonger (backs); Coles, McPherson and Norris (halves); Capes [1], Calvey [1], Beveridge, Morris and Spouncer (forwards).
Referee: Mr. Scragg (Crewe)

Bury's late comeback against a Notts. side that seemed to have the game 'in the bag' from the early minutes was a remarkable achievement for the "Shakers" but a bitter pill to swallow for those connected with the Foresters. Indeed, upon referee Mr. Scragg ordering extra-time to be played he had been approached upon the field by Mr. Hallam, the Nottingham club secretary, who, no doubt realising the Bury team were in the ascendancy at that point, strongly argued against the continuation of the match, but was instructed to leave the field. Then, after the conclusion of the extra period, which had indeed resulted in Bury's victory, Mr. Hallam had sought out Mr. Scragg in the dressing-room and, according to the latter, had harangued and insulted him. Mr. Scragg reported the incident to the F.A. whilst the Forest club declared it's intention to lodge a formal protest against the result of the match on the grounds that Mr. Scragg had had no authority to take the match into extra time - such an eventuality not having been clearly mandated by the F.A. and communicated to both clubs before the start. Mr. Hallam subsequently travelled to London to personally file the complaint at F.A. headquarters, but after talking 'off the record' with certain members of the Association (who perhaps indicated to him the wisdom of not calling further attention to his own conduct in the matter) thought better of the action and returned to Nottingham with the document still in his possession.

MILLWALL v. SOUTHAMPTON
at Crystal Palace, London – Saturday 24th March, 1900
Sports Argus - Saturday 24th March, 1900

The meeting of Millwall and Southampton this afternoon aroused vast interest in the South of England, and although it somewhat reduces the neutral character of the ground to play semi-finals there, the Crystal Palace enclosure was undoubtedly the proper one to select. Millwall are, of course, much nearer to it than Southampton, but from our little experience of the journey from the Isle of Dogs we should almost prefer the long one from Southampton. At any rate, it was the wish of both clubs to play at the Palace, and it will be a stiff battle. Southampton selected Buxton as their training quarters. This is rather singular, considering the many Health Resorts adjacent to London. Millwall, like Bury, were content to remain at home, and do their "spins" ascending the thousand-odd steps at Blackwall tunnel. Up to the present they are perfectly satisfied with the course of training, and certainly against Aston Villa, at Reading, they were hard as nails. They are not a scientific team, and don't claim to be, but they undoubtedly perform on cup tie lines. So far as can be made out, both clubs will have teams fully representative, and, with the single exception of Turner, the whole of the Southampton players have at one time or another been connected with League clubs. The Millwall directors have been doing all in their power to combine pleasure with work during the past week. On Thursday the men witnessed "The Messenger Boy" at the Gaiety Theatre, and last night they were at Daly's to see Yen How's six little wives in "San Toy." After today's hurly-burly the team will visit either the Empire, the Palace Theatre, or the Hippodrome. Southampton travelled from Buxton last night, and put up at the Crystal Palace Hotel, West Norwood. They were all fit as fiddles, and modestly confident, although it was recognized that they had nothing to give away. They were all fit as fiddles, and modestly confident, although it was recognized that they had nothing to give away. The team will be the same that has done duty in the three previous games with one exception. With Farrell restored to health again, Roddy McLeod has had to fall out as reserve centre, and although in the light of his accomplishments against Newcastle and the Throstles this seems to be rather hard on the old Albionite, it must be remembered that Farrell is a younger man, and with equal skill is the more likely to last against such a wearing side as Millwall.

A keen Nor'easter was blowing and 40,000 spectators were present at the commencement of the game. A great shout greeted the winning of the toss by Millwall, who had the benefit of a strong breeze to help them. Punctually to time, with the teams as advertised, Southampton kicked off. The Londoners left wing quickly made an incursion, towards which the half-back Miller assisted. A foul against this player gave Southampton a free kick. Some exchanges in the centre of the field followed. Wood and Milward went right in front of Cox, but the ball was sent behind. A foul by Chadwick gave them a free kick inside the halfway line. It was beautifully placed by Burgess, and the ball dropped in front of Robinson. An exciting rally occurred after the goal had been cleared, and a neat header was sent close in. The seasiders certainly were the quicker on the ball, the half-backs backing up the forwards splendidly, giving the Millwall defence a lot of trouble. Burgess did a deal of good work. Robinson next grandly saved a hot shot from Brierley. In turn, both goalkeepers were threatened. Cox conceded a corner, and Robinson intercepted a well meant centre. Fouls were frequent, and the only combination, or approach to it, was made by the Soton left wing. The greasy state of the turf precluded any very noticeable short passing work, and the full-backs repeatedly returned the long volleys, both sets of forwards playing ragged football. Banks did good single handed work for Millwall, but the half-backs dominated the situation. After very even play a miskick by Allen let in Wood, after a clean run down the field, causing Cox to leave his goal. He just got the ball first, and averted danger. A second later he fisted out a long dropping shot. The ball then visited the Southampton end, to be speedily returned, Milward making a pretty run along the wing. Working to the Southampton half, Robinson several times exhibited resourceful and powerful kicking. Eventually the ball went behind, and from the goal kick Southampton shot high up, but the keeper saved splendidly. Southampton again broke away, the three inside men going up in a heap. They hampered each other, and the final shot was very weak. Quickly working it down again in front of Robinson, Dryburgh gave Banks a fine chance close in, but he sent high over the bar. Give and take play again followed. Millwall showed little combination, and were repeatedly penalised for fouling, fully ten free kicks being awarded during as many minutes. The ball, however, was never near goal until Banks shot in. Millwall attacked, but there was little combination about their work. Millwall came through and centred, but Yates deliberated too long, and he was robbed of the ball. Brierley shot right into Robinson's hands, Millwall being awarded a free kick. Half-time: Millwall Athletic, nil; Southampton, nil.

On changing ends, almost as soon as the ball moved Allen made a bad mistake, letting in the Southampton forwards. They skirmished around Cox's charge, until Wood and Burgess, in trying to head the ball simultaneously, collided forcibly, both being hurt, and the game was stopped. The breeze was now telling in the seasiders favour. Play was taken out of Millwall's hands by a foul against Chadwick. A long kick by Durber returned it. Play was rough and ready. Nicol centred across the Southampton goalmouth, but nobody was up to receive it. Backward again the leather travelled, and Farrell and Yates got close in to Cox, but finding no opening, sent the ball back to Meston, and the latter put over. It was anybody's game now, and science was at a discount. Goldie, Millwall's centre-half, kicked Yates in the back, and the crowd vehemently hooted. Nicoll made a fine run along the wing, and shots were sent in left and right at Robinson, who excelled himself. A foul against Southampton gave Millwall a free kick at 40 yards range, but nothing resulted. Excitement was at boiling pitch. Banks was severely hurt, and a foul against Millwall immediately followed. After Banks retired, with 10 men, Millwall still held their own well, Burgess playing a great game. Banks returned, and received a great welcome. Several of Millwall's shots were repelled, and the ball was sent behind. A free kick 20 yards off the Millwall goal was attended with a like result. The referee was very keen on fouls, of which there were enough and to spare. Cox just saved from Farrell by giving a corner, which was ineffectual. Gettins was hurt, coming in contact with Chadwick. After a lot of midfield play Wood and Milward worked their way down, but the latter sent behind. The same player got in a brilliant shot from the corner flag, which Cox saved well, a performance which he repeated a minute later. Southampton pressing Dryburgh relieved with a touchline run.

RESULT: Millwall 0 – Southampton 0

SOUTHAMPTON: Robinson (goal); Durber and Meehan (backs); Petric, Chadwick and Meston (halves); Turner, Yates, Farrell, Wood and Milward (forwards).
MILLWALL: Cox (goal); Burgess and Allan (backs); Smith, Goldie and Millar (halves); Dryburgh, Brierley, Gettins, Banks and Nicholl (forwards).
Referee: Mr. A. Kingscott (Derby)

MILLWALL v. SOUTHAMPTON (Replay)
at Elm Park, Reading – Saturday 24th March, 1900
Daily Telegraph and Courier - Saturday 24th March, 1900
FOOTBALL ASSOCIATION CUP. SOUTHAMPTON v. MILLWALL.

Southampton and Millwall replayed their tie in the semi-final round of the competition for the Association Cup at Reading yesterday, when a game in which the Southampton men displayed far greater skill than the representatives of Millwall ended in favour of the Hampshire club by 3 goals to 0. The question of which of these teams should qualify for participation in the concluding stage of the struggle for possession of the national trophy was of comparatively small importance compared with the necessity for something being done to rehabilitate the reputation of South-country Association football - so badly damaged at the Crystal Palace last Saturday - and it is extremely satisfactory to be able to state that the winners gained the day by sheer merit.

Early in the contest Millwall were several times pulled up for fouls, but yesterday Southampton did not allow themselves to be put off their game. With the ground in very fair condition, and scarcely any wind blowing, the Millwall men seemed to make up their minds from the start that their only chance of success lay in the possibility of upsetting the combination of their opponents. For a long time they attempted little or nothing in the way of a concerted attack, being much more concerned in breaking up that of Southampton. These tactics had proved most effective at the Palace, when the fresh breeze had interfered somewhat with the accuracy of the Southampton passing, and after a while the Hampshire club had become, if not demoralised, at least almost resigned to the necessity of answering rigour with vigour, and abandoning the niceties of the game. No such complaint could be urged against Southampton yesterday. From the first they set to work in very pretty fashion, skilfully avoiding, whenever possible, collisions with their antagonists, and for twenty minutes after the kick-off play was largely in the Millwall half. Occasionally, after repelling an attack, the London team would break away, but they generally had the ball soon taken from them, and at other times kicked far too hard. Very different was it with Southampton, who repeatedly threatened danger. Milward and Wood, on the left wing, seemed to have an almost perfect understanding and Turner, on the other aide of the ground, made some dashing runs. In the early stages of the match Burgess proved a tower of strength to his side, checking one attack after another, and kicking the ball back towards mid-field. Once Gettins dashed away, but Meehan stopped him finely, this being almost the only occasion during the first twenty minutes that Millwall looked at all like scoring, whereas their opponents were repeatedly dangerous. After Turner had been temporarily laid out, and other fouls had been given against Millwall, there came further pressure on the London club's goal, and when the game had been in progress nearly half an hour **Milward**, dribbling down, at last beat Burgess, and shooting close in, scored the first point for Southampton. Within the next minute Wood only just missed increasing that cub's lead, and a moment later, with Millwall breaking away, Gettins sent in a stinging shot, which had it gone a foot or so lower, would have severely tested even Robinson's powers of defence. This piece of work roused Millwall to better work than they had previously shown. Twice in rapid succession Robinson had long shots to clear, and then Chadwick fouling an opponent, the Hampshire club's goal was again in great jeopardy. Other attacks ensued, and two corners to Millwall resulted, but nothing came of them. Soon Southampton were again holding the upper hand. Wood being fouled, the free kick nearly took effect, Chadwick putting over after Burgess had saved. Then Farrell and Wood got away but a misunderstanding between them at the finish saved Millwall. Before the interval, Milward, Wood, and Yates all had shots at the Millwall goal, and those of the two first were within an ace of scoring, inasmuch as, had they gone just under instead of just over the bar, could scarcely have got to them. When half-time arrived, however, Southampton had to be content with a lead of 1 goal to none.

Southampton at once settled down to pretty work on resuming and soon there came a most exciting bully right in the Millwall goal mouth, eight or ten of the players being hopelessly mixed up for several seconds. Eventually the referee blew his whistle and gave Stillwell a free kick - though for what reason onlookers were quite unable to see. Still came one attack after another on the Millwall posts, but sometimes Cox fisted out, and once or twice he was properly impeded. Within a quarter of an hour of the resumption Millwall were penalised for a foul in the Southampton half. Meehan taking the kick, the ball was passed on to **Milward**, who cleverly headed into the net, and so scored Southampton's second goal. Having gained so substantial a lead, Southampton dropped back for a time, and it must be admitted that in their efforts to check Millwall they were several times guilty of breaches of the rules, which called for and received the notice of the referee. Robinson however, was delightfully cool, and fisted away almost as far as an ordinary kick. In the midst of much pressure by Millwall their opponents once got away, and Farrell, passing out to Milward, the latter had very bad luck, hitting the upright with Cox a yard or so away. Instead of going into the net, the ball went the other side of the post, and so Millwall temporarily escaped. Other fouls were given against Southampton, and once when Robinson was trying to clear Gettins nearly beat him. Just at the end Southampton, confident of success, played a more open game, and Milward centreing, the ball hit Farrell and went to **Yates**, who promptly put it between the posts. Less than a minute then remained for play, and when the end came Southampton could claim a well-deserved victory.

After Saturday's match, yesterday's game, at Reading, came as a most refreshing change. Millwall certainly never arrived at any pitch of excellence in attack, the left wing being deplorably tame, and neither Gettins nor the right wing being up to form. Smith and Millar worked hard at half, but were not always successful, while at back Burgess tackled strenuously and well throughout. The best feature of the Southampton game was the skilful passing between Milward and Wood. Farrell failed to realise expectations, and Turner, after being badly fouled, did not continue as well as he had commenced. Chadwick did grand work at half-back, and shared the honours of the game with Milward. He tackled skilfully and fearlessly, and fed his men with excellent judgment. Possessed of so much ability, it was a pity that at times he descended to tricks which compelled the referee to give several fouls against him. Meehan kicked hard and well, and received useful support from Durber, while Robinson was, as usual, an admirable goalkeeper. Southampton, by their victory yesterday, earned the right to play either Bury or Nottingham Forest - whichever win today - at Crystal Palace in the Final tie on April 21. They can claim to be the first south country club to have reached the concluding stage since the Old Etonians played and lost to Blackburn Olympic in 1883.

RESULT: Millwall 0 – Southampton 3

SOUTHAMPTON: Robinson (goal); Durber and Meehan (backs); Petrie, Chadwick and Meston (halves); Turner, Yates [1], Farrell, Wood and Milward [2] (forwards).
MILLWALL: Cox (goal); Burgess and Allan (backs); Smith, Goldie and Millar (halves); Dryburgh, Brierley, Gettins, Banks and Nicholl (forwards).
Referee: Mr. A. Kingscott (Derby)

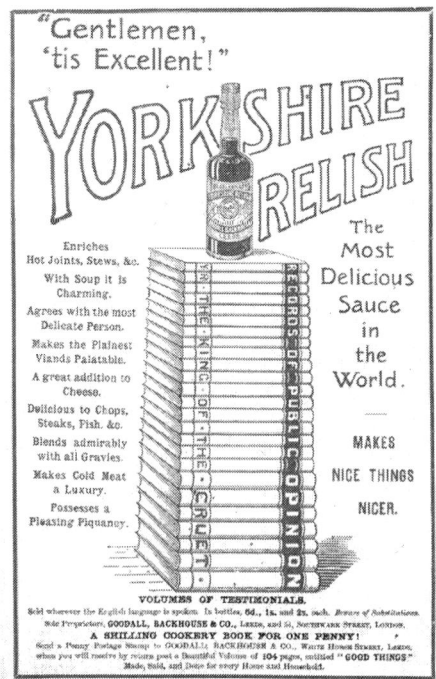

1899/1900 - Final

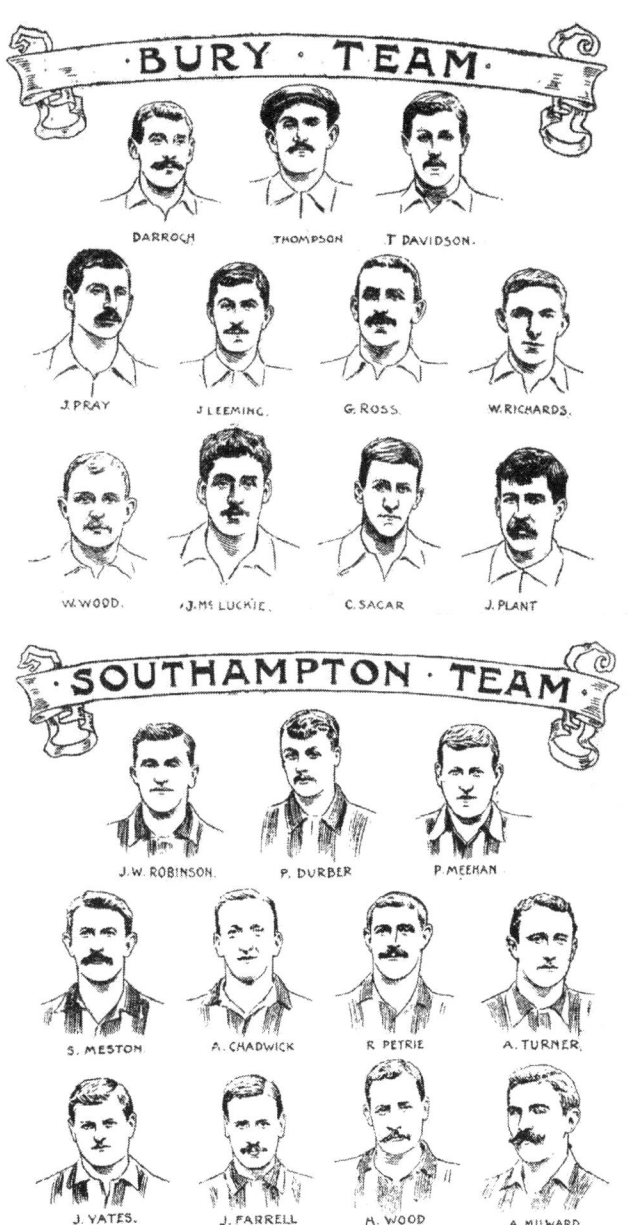

Player Comparisons

Name	Nat.	Age	Height	Weight	Position	Weight	Height	Age	Nat.	Name
Thompson	EN	24	5'8½"	11/4	Goal	13/2	5'10"	34	EN	Robinson
Darroch	SC	27	5'8"	11/3	Right Back	13/10	5'9½"	26	SC	Meehan
Davidson	SC	25	5'11½"	12/9	Left Back	11/5	5'8"	26	EN	Durber
Pray	SC	25	5'9"	12/10	Right Half	12/0	5'10"	29	SC	Meston
Leeming	EN	24	5'9"	11/0	Centre Half	12/2	5'8"	31	EN	Chadwick
Ross	SC	30	5'6½"	12/2	Left Half	11/0	5'7"	28	SC	Petrie
Richards	EN	21	5'7"	11/0	Outside Right	11/8	5'8"	23	EN	Turner
Wood	EN	21	5'7"	11/4	Inside Right	11/0	5'6"	30	EN	Yates
McLuckie	SC	21	5'11½"	12/12	Centre Forward	11/2	5'8"	26	EN	Farrell
Sagar	EN	22	6'0"	11/7	Inside Left	13/3	5'9½"	32	EN	Wood
Plant	EN	28	5'8"	12/0	Outside Left	11/3	5'7½"	30	EN	Milward
		24	5'9"	11/9	Average	11/13	5'8½"	29		

THE GOALKEEPERS

BURY: FRED THOMPSON, the goalkeeper, is an Englishman, and learned his job under the famous Doig, of Sunderland, on Good Friday, 1895. He was, with Sunderland's consent, signed by the Shakers, and played for them in 1896. Since then he has done first rate work with his present team, though he never replaced Montgomery, the regular Bury custodian, until this season. He is clever, and saves in all the most improved style, and is a great favourite.

SOUTHAMPTON: JOHN W. 'Jack' ROBINSON, the custodian, is a well known man wherever Association football is played. He made his name and fame with Derby County, where, along with Goodall, he was located many seasons, and during which time he gained the greatest honours possible, a number of caps against Scotland. In all Robinson has played in nine International games, the latest being the fateful one against Scotland this month. He first appeared for Lincoln City, then for Derby County, then New Brighton, and lastly and presently with Southampton.

THE RIGHT BACKS

BURY: The right full back of the side is a Scotsman from the famous football district, Vale of Leven, in Dumbartonshire. His name is **JOHN 'Jack' DARROCH**, and he is 27 years of age. He began his football career with the Old Vale team which was scattered by the English clubs appearing with the Sheffield Wednesday team in 1891. Three years later he returned to Scotland, this time playing with Dundee, and before joining the Bury team he played in the famous semi-final for the Scottish Cup, when Renton and Dundee met three times. Jack, as he is familiarly styled, signed for Bury four seasons ago, and at that time partnered the old warhorse Banham, who did so much to make the name of the Bury team famous. Darroch is a fearless but withal an honest player, and has the respect of all his opponents. He stands half an inch less than the custodian.

SOUTHAMPTON: PETER MEEHAN, the right full back, has been a rolling-stone. A Scotsman, he has long been in the land of he Southron, and has seen service with Sunderland and Everton prior to joining the Southampton organisation. He has also been a tried and trusted man in the ranks of the Celtic of Glasgow. He has never had the distinction of gaining the cap which all his compatriots long for (English), but he has done duty for Scotland against Ireland. He is a rattling and fearless defender, and game to the last minute of the play.

THE LEFT BACKS

BURY: THOMAS DAVISON, the Bury left full-back, is also a Scotsman, coming to the Shakers from Dyke Head Club, a minor Lancashire organisation. He was one of the men whom the club secured when they were just emerging from the juniordom in 1894-5 or the season they left the Lancashire League for the Second Division of the League, and, by the way, the club only remained a member of the probationary body one season. Davidson can play either right or left back, but prefers his present position, and always plays his best game there. He's a rattling tackler, fair if vigorous, and often extricates his side from tight places.

SOUTHAMPTON: PETER DURBER, the left full back, is an Englishman, and a rattling man in his place. His tackling is judicious, his kicking strong, and when pushed he is one of the hardest men to beat it is possible to find. He made his reputation with the Stoke club, and was a much admired man by many of the League clubs prior to falling a victim to the allurements of the Saints. He is not an International, but has appeared in the North and South match on behalf of the South this season. He played well, but did not catch the judge's eye.

THE RIGHT HALVES

BURY: JOHN PRAY, who occupies the right half back position, has been captain of the team for three seasons, and there is not a man on the whole side who would not go through a lot at the call of his skipper, who always set a good example by hard work himself. He is a native of Falkirk, Scotland. He was, before joining the Bury club, a clubmate of Montgomery when the pair wore the colours of the Glasgow Rangers, and used to please the crowds at Ibrox park. He has been with Bury five years, and has had the good fortune to play in almost all games for five seasons, the loss per winter being not more than a couple.

SOUTHAMPTON: SAMUEL MESTON, the right half back, is a bit of a wonder. He is the oldest playing member of the team, being twenty nine years of age. He is, however, still nimble as a cat, and if a bit of a veteran, he is spry enough for many of the forwards knocking about today. Before joining the unattached ranks, i.e. joining a club outside the League, Meston was a playing member of Stoke, and was one of the men about whom their was a bother, or rather boycotting[11], which the League had to abandon. Still the jews do not mix with the gentiles.

---

11 The F.L. had temporarily banned their members from arranging fixtures with S.L. clubs over a row concerning the poaching of players from the North to the South.

THE CENTRE HALVES

BURY: JOSEPH LEEMING, the centre half of the team, in is a Prestonian, and learned how to do his work by studying the methods of the famous old North End Club. He was born in the proud town and made the famous Sandy Robertson his model, and did well off him. He first made his mark as a player with the Edgeworth school team, who played at Turton, near Bolton. He then joined the Turton team, a club which, by the way, gave the world the present chairman of the football league, Mr. J.J. Bentley, and from thence migrated to Bury, taking up his position there in the season 1897-8. He did duty as a reserve man that season, but this winter he thoroughly earned his place at centre half.

SOUTHAMPTON: ARTHUR CHADWICK, the centre-half of the team, is a Lancashire lad. He is a brother of the Edgar Chadwick of Everton fame, and presently at Burnley. He also has another brother who is making himself known to the world in the role of a referee. Arthur is a rattling man in his position, and although he did happen to be one of those in the fateful 4-1 beating England sustained lately, if all the men had done as well as he, well the result would have been quite different. He was born at Accrington, and played with the now defunct Reds. He then went to Burton Swifts, and later to Southampton, where he is held in high esteem. He has played in the eleven three seasons.

THE LEFT HALVES

BURY: GEORGE ROSS, the senior member of the team, is a Scotsman by birth, but has spent all but twelve of months of his life in Lancashire. Ross *pere* was a constable, and left his native place to join the Lancashire County Constabulary. From Preston the family migrated to Bury, where some sixteen or seventeen years ago George began playing football with the Bury Wesleyan club. He was not long in seclusion, joining the Bury club some twelve years ago, before even the organisation became connected with the Lancashire League. He has for all this dozen years been a steady and consistent player. "Men may come, and men may go, but George goes on for ever," they have begun to say in Bury. He has played in practically every match since his club got into the First Division of the League. He's getting on, for he has reached thirty, but there is yet a lot of good football in him.

SOUTHAMPTON: The left half back is **ROBERT PETRIE**, Scotsman. He was born in Dundee in 1877, and played for Dundee when first they were admitted to the Scottish League Division One. He subsequently migrated to Sheffield, where he played in the ranks of the Wednesday with credit to his club. He was one of the Wednesday's cup eleven when they carried off the trophy, and is expected to get another gold medal because Southampton won today. He is a willing and capable worker and never tires. His feeding is really fine.

THE OUTSIDE RIGHTS

BURY: WILLIAM 'Billy' RICHARDS, the outside right, is another Lancashire lad. He was born at Heaton Park, and at the age at 18 played for Middleton Parish Church. He subsequently joined Tonge, a Lancashire Alliance eleven, and then migrated to play for Middleton in the Lancashire League. He was tried by Bury at the end of last season, facing the Bolton Wanderers defence. He came off, and was signed on a League form. He began playing regularly with the team this season after October came in, and has done good service ever since.

SOUTHAMPTON: A TURNER, the outside right, is the only Hampshire man in the team - rather a disappointing statement to have to make. But if he is the only one he is a rattler. In his place there are few men who can equal him, and still fewer who can beat him. He is tricky, clever, and can centre accurately, and when the opportunity offers he can let the opposing goalkeeper have something to be going along with. He has secured his "cap" this season against Ireland, and has also taken part in the North v. South match, in the ranks of the latter. He has also done duty for Hampshire and the Southern League. He is one of the most promising players of the year.

THE INSIDE RIGHTS

BURY: WILLIAM WOOD, who partners Richards on the right, is another Middleton lad, and has, therefore, always been a club mate of his present partner. Singular to relate however, when the pair have formed the Middleton right wing their positions were the reverse of what they are now. He joined Bury at the end of last season, and partnered Settle, now of Everton. He was badly injured at the beginning of the present season, and was absent from ten games.

SOUTHAMPTON: JAMES YATES, the inside right, made his name when playing under the banner of Sheffield United, but has done really fine work for the Saints. He joined his present club in 1898, and played for them one season. Subsequently, or rather last season, he played under the colours of the Gravesend club, but he could not settle down, and consequently returned this season to the Saints. He is speedy, and when he gets a pass from his partner knows what to do with the ball; at least, the opposing custodians think he does as a rule.

THE CENTRE FORWARDS

BURY: JAMES McLUCKIE, one of the tallest men in the team, and is, of course, a Scotsman. His native place being Glasgow. He is twenty-one years of age, and joined Bury at the commencement of the season 1998-9, prior to which he played for Jordan Hill, a junior team. He was only promoted to a regular place in the first team towards the end of last season, but since then he has done good service. He is just a shade under 6 foot high.

SOUTHAMPTON: JOHN FARRELL, the centre, is a man worthy of his place. He is a Shropshire youth, and made his name and fame in the ranks of the Stoke club. He was born at Tunstall, in Staffordshire, and is twenty-seven years of age. As a centre he plays an ideal game. He never leaves his men to help themselves, but keeps them in close touch, and the manner in which he slips the ball to one or the other - whichever is in the best position - is one of the most interesting items to watch during a game in which he is figuring.

THE INSIDE LEFTS

BURY: CHARLES SAGAR, the inside man of the team is another member of the old Turton Club. He began his football career with the Turton St. Anne's Sunday School Club, then members of the Bolton and District Sunday School. He later on played for Turton and in April, 1898, took up his post in the Bury organisation. Since then he has rapidly come to the front. He was selected as reserve man for England against Scotland last season. As a matter of fact he has played one international game this season against Ireland, and scored one of the goals.

SOUTHAMPTON: HARRY WOOD is a Staffordshire lad, coming from Wolverhampton, though he was born at Walsall. He was, up to joining the saints three seasons ago, the shining light of the Midlands. He had taken all the honour it is possible for a man to get. He has an English Cup medal and International caps galore - in fact, Harry, who is a most unpretentious man, is one of the best known who has ever kicked a ball. He is the captain of the Saints, and "a right good captain too." His men will do anything for him. He is thirty-two years of age, but for all that is plenty speedy enough for a fast forward rank, for what he cannot do in the way of sprinting he can accomplish by passing and a bit of finesse.

THE OUTSIDE LEFTS

BURY: JOHN 'JACK' PLANT junior, the outside left, this season gained his cap against Scotland, and though the team got one of the worst drubbings in history, it was not Plant's fault. Plant is a Cheshire Lad, having been born at Bollington, near Macclesfield, and played with the Bollington Club prior to joining Bury some ten years ago. Until the season 1897-8 Plant was a regular member of the Bury team, but he then took a fit for a change, and played for Reading in the season 1898-9, but he came home again this season and has done good work for the team. He has participated in all Bury's big games, and is proud of his team.

SOUTHAMPTON: ALFRED MILWARD is another Lancashire player. He really belongs to the South, but he was developed in Lancashire, and as long as ever the dribbling code is played so long will the famous Chadwick-Millward wing of the Everton club be talked about. The pair could simply outwit and outdistance any defence once they gained possession of the ball. Ask many of Scotland's ablest defenders about them, also enquire of many League defenders. But Everton threw off Millward as "done up" two seasons ago. He then joined New Brighton, but joined Southampton this season, and is just about as good as ever he was, and if the Saints don't win the cup today it won't be Alf's fault.

The two teams were very evenly matched in terms of height and weight, and whereas with an average age of 24 to Southampton's 29 Bury may have had the pull in terms of youth and vitality, Southampton had, by all appearances at least, the counter in terms of craft and experience. In fact in goalkeeper Jack Robinson and forwards Harry Wood and Alf Milward they had three of the best known and most experienced men in the country. The stage, it seemed, was set for a battle of graft versus guile.

Before the Match

The Bury team left for London at 9.00 o'clock on Thursday morning (19th April) to be put up at the Tavistock Hotel in Covent Garden until their return the following Monday, the Directors lodging separately at the Royal Crystal Palace Hotel.

On the day of the match thousands of enthusiasts trained in from the provinces, the largest numbers of course coming from Lancashire and Hampshire but all the major centres being to some extent represented. The major railway companies, indeed, providing: Midland Railway, 18 specials; Great Central Railway, 18 Specials; London and North Western Railway, 15 specials; Great Northern Railway, 11 specials; London and South Western Railway, 6 specials; Other lines, 8 (approx) specials.

The weather on the day of the match was that of an ideal summer day for sport – clear and bright, with a gentle breeze alleviating the worst of the heat of a broiling Sun unabated in a cloudless sky. Only a few day's previously, on Easter Monday, the Corinthians had played a game on the same ground in typically wintry conditions of rain and snow showers. On the road's leading to the Crystal Palace before the match the red and white colours of the Sotonians seemed to predominate everywhere, in favours, clothing and banners, the dark blue and white of Bury being, perhaps, not so much less prominent as less striking.

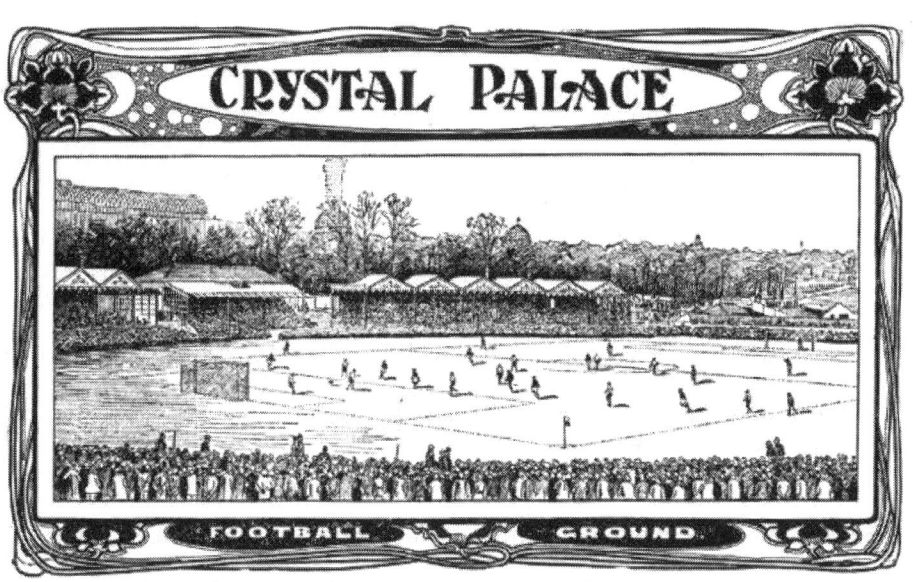

BURY v. SOUTHAMPTON
st Crystal Palace, London – Saturday 21st April, 1900
Sporting Life - Monday 23 April 1900
SOUTHAMPTON OUT OF THEIR ELEMENT.
CROWD AND BRILLIANT WEATHER.

What a hold football has on the masses! The "Final Tie" appears to exercise the same infatuation over the true enthusiasts as does a pilgrimage to Mecca by all devout Mahommedans. London falls temporarily into the clutches of the provincial excursionists, keen and untiring in the pursuit of the pleasure to be derived from the chaotic strugglings, tremendous perseverance, and general athletic doings of twenty-two young men within the limits of an ever to be talked of ninety stirring minutes. On Saturday London was overrun by lusty-toned Lancashire lads, the blue and white favours of Bury denoting their partisanship and locating the centre from whence they had travelled. How keenly these toilers from the County Palatine interested themselves in the well doing of the team they had journeyed - before the dawn had broken - these hundreds of miles to cheer and support. It was the same expression of feeling from all of them, "Ten years since t'coop came to Lancashire, tha knows. We want it again." No use to point out that for nigh on twenty long not a Southern club had attained the dignity of being a finalist. All the heartburnings of those successive year, the taunts we of the South had received from the all-conquering Northerners, that not even the rudiments of scientific football were vouchsafed to us, that by an unwritten law the Cup - that unimpressive but glorious piece of silverware - was the property of the great League clubs handed one to the other season to season as the Fates so willed it, did not appeal to the hard-headed Lancashire folk. Sentiment was a1togother lacking with them. If there was any it was concentrated on the side of Bury, for Southampton not one iota. We have concurred since their overcoming of Millwall that the Southampton team was actually representative of the best football talent at the disposal the South of England. Leading to their success in the semi-final, they had in turn beaten three First League combinations - Everton, Newcastle United, and West Bromwich Albion. Victories indicative, indeed, of the quality of Southampton's Cup fighters. From the day that the pair of finalists had emerged from the trials and troubles which gave them the right to meet in the all important contest at the Crystal Palace the partisans of the South have been in a perfect fever of expectancy. Could it only happen? Could or would Southampton win the Cup? The vexed question troubled one day and night. As the day approached it was seen with absolute sorrow that Southampton were trailing off. Their Southern League matches, in which they turned out at full strength against Thames Ironworks and Tottenham Hotspur, were something of fiascos. Excuses were made, but it was very patent that a lapse of form had occurred: the long season's hard work was telling its irresistible tale. Had the final tie been contested some three weeks back matters might wear a brighter aspect for Southern partisans than they do now. The scenes by road and rail befitted the occasion. Train load after train load of packed and perspiring humanity steamed away from London into the sunny suburbs. It can well be said that "all roads lead to the Palace." Four-in-hands, the London "Gondola" motor cars[12], and the ubiquitous cycle ported their freight to the centre of attraction - the Crystal Palace. The coach of the non-commissioned officers of the Guards was

---

12   Taxi cabs. The horse-drawn hansom cab was once described by Prime Minister Disraeli as 'the Gondola of London' but had by this time been largely replaced by the motorised variety.

conspicuous by it's surmounting scarlet blazing in the generous sunshine. Through the leafy - so in reality - glades to Sydenham the stream of vehicles seemed to be unending. A holiday, indeed, in the bright fresh air with the great struggle for the Cup thrown in. The Palace itself was early on astir with many thousands the tramping of many feet resounded through the great building. Like a vast hot-house it received and retained the rays of a most powerful sunshine. To reach the beautiful gardens already putting on their garment was to marvel at the heat. Football on such a day really savoured of desecration. A Midsummer day forsooth in the middle of April. The shade of friendly nooks and trees were as welcome as was this, the balmy breath of Summer. Round and about the grounds the party colours were much in evidence. An hour before the kick off the crowd on the banking on the south side of the arena had assumed larger proportions. Right and left of it, too, was being filled up steadily and surely. The undulating slopes leading from the Palace, which loomed large over all, glinting and flashing involuntary Helios[13] in the sunshine, sent down an unceasing stream of people. From paths, from around trees, wheeling and circling they ever came to swell the multitude below. Swelteringly did King Sol repay those who had taken their positions. Patiently, however they bore it. Around iron railings bounding the football field the crowd was compactly pressed. Behind and above them, with more breathing room, patriotic songs were much and vigorously discussed by the good-humoured waiting assemblage. An operator with a cornet kept them in time and tune, a most respectable volume of sound being disgorged as the burden of each refrain rose on the clear air. Cheer upon cheer followed in the wake of each rendering, and altogether the time did not hang too heavily on the devoted enthusiasts heads. Across the bright even turf the background of stands bordering the Southern portion of the ground looked heavy and dull. They were not at this point half filled, most of their future occupants being occupied in promenading the field. A turn or two over the greensward showed the turf to be very firm, and that - as had been officially notified - the usual area of the playing field had been considerably modified. Both from the width and length some eight feet had been deducted. This proceeding was taken in deference to the wishes of both teams as bringing the delimitation somewhere approaching that of their own ground. Half an hour prior to the advertised time of the game commencing a full band, resplendent in scarlet and gold, enlivened the stands and Pavilion occupants, with popular selections, winding up finally with "Rule Britannia" and "God Save the Queen." With one accord hats went off, and that stirring, moving spectacle of thousands of Englishmen standing bareheaded and sending forth the National Hymn was seen. A minute or two later a burst of hand clapping from within the Pavilion, denoted some noteworthy arrival. It was Lord Rosebery, throwing aside convention by wearing a straw hat, accompanied by his eldest son, Lord Dalmeny, similarly seeking protection from the sun's rays, which now seemed stronger than ever. The ring of spectators rose at his lordship. The minutes still to elapse before the start were occupied by the rival teams being photographed in the Pavilion, and the occupying of every available vantage point overlooking the football arena. A tremendous array of heads met the eye as it swept it's gaze around. Tier upon tier they seemed to surmount each other till the sky-line of azure blue dominated the topmost rows. Packed like sardines they seemed to be a veritable vast multitude all of which could not fairly be seen, for in subtle recesses of the trees on the upper part of the embankments groups were half hid away. Into the trees and swaying high aloft, like ornaments on gigantic Christmas trees, adventurous

---

13 Helios – Greek God of the sun.

youths had clambered by the score. A sudden shout from all parts of the ground took the glance away to other parts. The Bury team, clad in white shirts and blue knickers, were in full career for the Western goal. Up went a miniature air balloon, showing the white and blue of the Lancashire club. It was uproariously greeted. An omen of good fortune it proved to be, plain and visible to all in the light, clear air. Southampton almost immediately came into view, and their reception was a truly grand one, and redolent of their supporters slogan of "Yi, yi, yi!" A brief spell of practice was indulged in, and then the presiding genius whistled the teams to prepare for the fray. Captains Harry Wood and Pray advanced to the mid-field line, and tossed for choice of ends. Much depended upon success in this respect, for a nice breeze came from behind the Western goal, and high in the heavens the fiery orb was darting its rays blindingly in its support. Woe to the side that had to face it's glamour. An uplifting of the hand, hasty glances on the ground pointing to the Western goal as his selection by Pray, and a chorus of exultation from the Lancashire visitors denoted that Southampton - the hope and pride of the South - had lost the toss.

Facing the brilliant sunshine and the freshening breeze stood the thin line of cherry and white shirts with their supporters, opposed to them the doughty, typical cup fighting lads from Bury. A shrill blast from the whistle and the ball and the players were on the move. The firm turf lent a volatility to the ball surprising to those whose connection with football has been in the months of winter when grounds are heavy and the atmosphere likewise, the ball went ahead as light as a feather. Very noticeable was this feature in the opening minutes of the contest. The half-backs were hopelessly at sea. Instead of feeding their front line, the ball invariably went on to the opposing defence or into touch. The pace of the ground quite upset Southampton's methods. Accustomed to play the short passing game, they appeared to have lost sight of the fact that the ball on holding turf can be placed with greater accuracy one man to another then when other conditions prevail. It was always running away from the players on Saturday. Time and again it struck the ground following the administering of a forcibly delivered kick, and rose to the height of a dozen feet so. Concerted work, or rather attempts at it, was sheer folly. Grasping the position in its proper light, the Bury men went in for individual tactics.

A dashing run by the wing men, a flying centre and a shot, a single-handed dribbling bout by their centre forward and a shot, and a hard kick ahead and a following of it up in the twinkling of eye by the inside men were the means adopted to best fit in with the necessities of the hour. They went straight through Southampton's defensive lines, half-backs right on the heels of the forwards, whenever, they got going. All the dash and go was with Bury, all the vacillation and deliberation, or, so it seemed to be, with Southampton. Ten minutes after the start a rush of the Bury front ranks found the International player, Chadwick, having a tussle on Southampton's goal-line with Wood, Bury's inside-right. The last named could not get in his centre, being hampered by the auburn haired Sotonian, but cunningly forced a corner off him. The corner-kick placed the ball right in the mouth of the Southampton goal. A brief striving and general chaos among the players there placed, and then **McLuckie,** Bury's tall centre forward, found the net. Running back to the centre of the field his hands were violently wrung by his nearest comrades, the while great shouts rent the air. For a while Southampton bothered their rivals, and Thompson in goal was seen dancing and crouching in the aperture as the cherry and white garments came closer and closer to him. Soon, however, the attack died away. Bury's pair of Internationals, Sagar and Plant, now gave Chadwick, Meston and Meehan a testing time of it. The Lancastrians had the pace of their men, and knew it. Their dashing sprints could not be stopped. Robinson made one lucky save from Sagar, the ball simply hitting the crack goalkeeper, who had no idea of its oncoming, such was its velocity at about ten yards range. A slight deviation from this procedure enabled Southampton to peregrinate[14] upon their opponents' half of the ground, Milward getting close in and hitting one of the uprights - a piece of ill luck. Promptly Bury resented this incursion, and Plant, assisted by his wing companion, careered towards Robinson at full tilt. Letting fly when well within range, the latter prevented the ball entering his charge, but the force of the impact was such that he fell to the ground. Some twelve yards into play the sphere travelled, and **Wood**, dashing up, sent it into the defenceless goal. Two goals in eighteen minutes! Well might the Northerners shout. At it again the Bury men were more determined than ever. Kick and rush, they were on and past in the twinkling of an eye. There seemed no barrier to these fierce, loose, but systematic rushes. Five minutes later **McLuckie**, receiving the ball from a half back, headed it over Meehan and Durber, who were attempting to block his path. Racing through the full-backs the centre forward had only Robinson to defeat to consummate a smart piece of work. Steadying himself beautifully for his shot he drove the ball along the ground into the corner of the net. Three goals in twenty-three minutes! The North-countrymen frantic with delight, the Southerners silent and awed by the disasters that had overtaken their champions. A general listlessness overcame the Sotonians, who now realised they had met their masters. Beyond a slight effort or two they did little of account, and with Bury saving themselves for the second portion nothing of interest from them had to be chronicled. At half-time the players retired for a well earned respite of ten minutes.

The sun and wind were expected to prove strong agents in Southampton's favour when the struggle was resumed. Neither had much effect, however, if the truth must be told. Certainly the superiority of Bury was not so strongly marked as in the previous portion, but was nevertheless manifestly assertive enough as to leave no doubts in impartial minds as to which was the better team on the day. McLuckie stood head and shoulders over the whole of the other belligerents in point of cleverness on the ball. He circumvented Chadwick adroitly, and caused the Southampton full-backs to hustle their burly bodies at an unwonted pace. He had them dead tired before the end. Towards the finish of the game, from which all real interest had long since departed, the Bury defending lines gave away several free kicks to their opponents, owing to infringements of the rules. Generally these occurred owing to the constant endeavours of the clever Sotonian left-wing, Wood and Millward, to get through. The last-mentioned was ever a willing trier, and did many clever things, but without avail. A quarter of hour or so before the close Pray sent in a long drive at Robinson, who just succeeded in keeping the ball out of the net by tipping it over the bar as the Bury forwards dashed up at him. From the corner-kick **Plant** was given a chance, and he made no mistake. Some minutes prior to the expiration of time, the crowd, which had thickly clustered on both sides of the pavilion, now swarmed on the field, which was a signal for those on the other side to join in the demonstration. However, they were soon cleared off, and only a slight stoppage in the proceedings thus occurred. Little variation in the conduct was seen,

---

14 Peregrinate [archaic] – to wander / to travel around on foot.

Bury playing the better game, and accomplishing the downfall of the Southern contingent absolutely and completely. A game to be mourned over till the proud day shall come when the south shall prevail. Four goals to nil! Was ever such discomfiture?

A DETAILED REPORT OF THE MATCH (from the same publication).

It was twenty eight minutes' past three when Pray having tossed, and beaten Wood, for choice of ends, took the west field and two minutes later Farrell started the game. Southampton had to face a brilliant sun, and also had the breeze against them. Commencing in business-like fashion Bury soon forced the pace, and Robinson was called upon to handle before play had been in progress a single minute. The burly custodian cleared correctly, and the ball going over to Turner, was at once transferred to neutral territory by that player. Chadwick, too, got a chance, and further improved the situation until the Lancashire backs robbed him. Plant was then responsible for a smart run down the wing, which terminated with an equally clever centre. Before McLuckie could reach the moving object Durber went to his side's assistance, and, passing forward, gave Farrell an opportunity of which he availed himself to run away with the ball at his toes. When he was tackled he transferred to the right and Turner again took up the running. He got right close up to the Bury goal, where he let fly, but, although the intention was good, the execution was upset by Darroch, who intercepted in the nick of time. It was a fine bit of play on the part of the Southampton right wing, and deserved a better fate, although to a great extent Turner was rewarded at the hands of the crowd. Scarcely a minute had elapsed when the Bury front rank forced their opponents to defend, and following good work on the part of the front line, Meehan had to heel back to Robinson in order that the ball might be cleared before the others swooped down on the goal. Once more Turner was in evidence, but this time distinguished himself in a somewhat different manner, inasmuch as he spoiled a good bit of combination by handling at the critical moment, and again the ball was returned to the Hampshire club's quarters. McLuckie was mainly responsible but, for the other side, just when he began to look extremely dangerous, Durber blocked further progress, and the front division attacked. The Southampton right wing received some slight accident to his knee, and had to retire temporarily. A capital understanding existing between Pray and his leading line of attack enabled Richards and Wood to gain a lot of ground, a shot from the latter being stopped by Robinson, who gave Chadwick a chance to show a bit of his cleverness. The football at this period had improved on the first few minutes of the game, and was interesting to watch, albeit excitement never ran high. Chadwick did a lot of good work for his side, but directly after he was unfortunately compelled to give a corner. Richards took the kick and nine minutes from the commencement **McLuckie** scored the first goal. The effort was a good one, and brought forth a howl of delight from the numerous partisans of the Bury team. As if to take an early revenge Farrell immediately led an onslaught into the opposition camp, and a regular melee in front of their goal ensued. It looked any odds on the South equalising, but although Milward went extremely close, the ball just dropped over. Thompson had a very lively ten seconds, and it must have been with a sigh of relief that he saw the effort abortive. A slight delay was caused through the Bury captain being hurt, but he was only incapacitated for a few minutes, and a little rubbing sufficed to send him into action again none the worse for colliding with an opponent. Indeed, he appeared to play all the better afterwards. Sagar and Plant between them carried hostilities to the

Sotonians end, and the services of Robinson were requisitioned. Kicking out to the left, Yates, who was evidently right off colour, gave over to his wing, and Turner dashed along until robbed by Ross, who in turn sent to Leeming when within shooting distance of the Southampton goal. The centre forward made his effort, but the ball went behind just a little wide of the posts. Following the goal-kick Plant was responsible for a capital run and centre to McLuckie, from which the latter gave the big Southern custodian more trouble. He was not the only one to worry Robinson, for both Wood and Sagar tried their luck, and although they both succeeded in hitting the human target, yet the ball was cleared with characteristic despatch. Returning to the other end a rather bad foul was given against Leeming, Farrell being the player to receive such unwelcome attention. Nothing, however, resulted from the kick, and although the South this time were having an equal share of the game, yet they were quite unable to break down the sturdy defence of the Bury posts. For a brief spell the ball hovered about in front of the Lancashire citadel, but Davidson saved the situation more than once, then Plant got possession and sent in a long shot which Robinson stopped well, but unfortunately for his side he could not get the ball quite away, and **Wood** coming up at the right moment rushed it through, thus putting Bury two goals up. Harry Wood next became prominent with a good attempt to beat Thompson, but the ball went over, and the next minute a similar bit of work at the other end on the part of Sagar met with an almost alike fate. The play of the Southerners, which had not been characterised by many bouts of combination, momentarily changed and Farrell and Turner, in co-operation with their captain attacked strongly, until Davidson went to his side's relief, and returned to the centre, from whence Wood gave the opposing defenders, trouble. The match was just twenty three minutes old when **McLuckie**, receiving a pass from Ross, headed over the heads of the backs, and following up, steadied himself, and then shot correctly past Robinson. A couple of minutes later Sagar kept up the pressure, and Plant very nearly put on another point, but the ball missed its mark. The Southerners now had what looked like a hopeless task on hand, but although half the life was knocked out of their play, yet they struggled on in the face of the broiling sun, and had quite enough to do when encountering the work of Wood. After playing for some time in the Bury end the venue was changed, and Robinson was just able to save from the Lancashire Wood, who found him a useful man to run against. Meston further improved the situation, and a cross shot from Turner gave Milward an opening, and the latter had the hard luck of seeing his shot hit the side of the net. Then followed a misunderstanding between Yates and Meston, which let in Sagar, who gained a lot of ground before being pulled up by Meehan. A corner to Southampton was cleared by McLuckie, and Pray soon after shot wide of the mark. Southampton then tried hard to score, and for a few minutes pressed, but Davidson again cleared, and Plant forced a corner which was effectually upset by Durber with a long high kick. Five minutes before the whistle sounded for half-time a visit to the Southern end terminated in Robinson saving cleverly from Richards, who put in a dropping shot. Then Plant caused some little trouble before Wood was able to get away with the ball at his toes. A couple of fouls against Southampton availed little, and a return was soon made to the Bury end where Farrell from an off-side position tested the ability of Thompson, and found him equal to the occasion. The whistle then sounded for the customary rest, the score reading: Bury, three goals; Southampton, nil.

A SNAPSHOT IN THE FOOTBALL FIELD: THE FINAL TIE FOR THE ASSOCIATION CUP AT THE CRYSTAL PALACE

NOT THE TOURBILLON DANCE, BUT A TRICKY BURY LEFT.

After a respite of just over ten minutes. McLuckie again set the ball in motion, and although they had the sun in their eyes, it was pretty clear to all present that such would not prevent the visitors from the North from continuing their successful career. Being pulled up by the backs, they had, however, to act decisively, and within only a minute or so Wood and Milward worked along the wing, and the latter headed past Thompson, but the ball failed to find the net. Then the Bury men once more got going, and matters were made particularly lively for their opponents. The ball was taken across the front, and both Sagar and Richards tried their luck, although without success. The Southerners, in response to advice freely given by their partisans, made several dashes, Chadwick being especially prominent. Once he sent the ball over the net, but although the effort was not a success, it was well intended, and was received with applause. Still, he played up well, and was, perhaps, the best of the bunch at this particular time. The play had sadly deteriorated, however, and the South were treating their supporters to anything but a good account of themselves. They absolutely went all to pieces, and even individual play worth noting was almost always conspicuous by its absence. The Bury men were very little better, but then it must be remembered that they had three good goals in hand, and all they had to do was to play a defensive game, and keep their goal intact. This they were not only enabled to do, but, as the sequel shows, they also managed to add further to the score. Ten minutes after the restart the Bury forwards made a dash, and, getting by the others' halves, McLuckie only missed scoring by a few feet. Following the goal-kick the Southerners made a half-hearted attack on their opponents preserves, but it was nevertheless sufficiently well maintained to get close to the Bury goal. Here one of the backs fouled Farrell, and wood shot just wide of the post. Following this attempt the ball was kept continually travelling up and down the field, one smart burst on the part of Turner being quite a relief to the general monotony of proceedings as they panned out. Bury continued to have the best of the argument, however, and Robinson was forced to concede a corner in endeavouring to clear a shot from the toe of McLuckie. Farrell got the ball away, and then ensued more play in the centre, from which neither side derived much benefit. The same player directly afterwards made a wide detour with the ball, terminating in a tricky run with a pass to Milward, who tried to save his side the ignominy of a blank sheet. The player had no time allowed for sighting purposes, so that although the ball failed to fulfil its intended mission, yet the effort was a good one, and had the effect of raising Southern supporters' drooping spirits. A couple of good runs on the part of Plant and Milward respectively gave the backs some little occupation, the latter player only being stopped by Davidson when close to the twelve yards line. With a long kick the ball was once again sent hying to the centre, from whence the forwards took it over into Southampton territory. Here a foul against the Saints very nearly let in Richards, and a sigh of relief went forth when Meehan at length cleared. The crowd were decidedly quiet, the followers of Southampton being utterly down in the mouth, whilst those of Bury were too full of joy at the successes already attendant on their favourites. With only twenty-five minutes to go, Plant made a further attempt to add to his glory, but the ball was taken from him ere his plan had matured, and the centre of the field was again the scene of operations. The game here was painfully slow, and audible remarks were to be heard as to the prevailing idea on the subject. Southampton were certainly stale, and one or two of them little more than passengers. Now end then, however, a burst was made, Farrell being responsible for a bit of decent play before being fouled close to the Bury goal. Nothing came of this kick, and immediately the Northerners paid a visit to the other end, where the ball was checked by Durber. Milward was badly tripped when he was going strong, but he nearly had revenge a little later, a shot of his just going over the crossbar. The Southampton front rank once more tried to combine, and accordingly gained ground, Milward being well to the fore whenever the ball went across to him. He was treated to a round of applause for his pains, but unfortunately try how he would the opposing backs were always in readiness to stop the attack. After more centre-field work, Yates, Turner, and Farrell bothered the Bury back for a while, but eleven minutes to the finish the Northerners forced a corner off Robinson, and Pray took the shot. He centred well in front of the net, and Plant added the fourth and last goal. With no possible chance of equalising the crowd gradually diminished, but a curious incident must not be forgotten. Mr. Kingscott had occasion to sound his whistle for a foul, and it being rather a longer signal than usual, the spectators trooped onto the pitch. The game, naturally, was stopped for a short time, but, on the referee's appeal, the ground was quickly cleared, and play was resumed, although not before a large number had wended their way towards the pavilion in anticipation of watching the presentation of the cup, which was to follow. The remaining seven minutes was not of the most interesting character, and indeed the end was welcome even to Southern supporters, who had had more than their fill, and a lot more than the least sanguine had bargained for. The victory was won fairly, and once again the cup will find a resting place in the North of England. The better side won, and they are fully entitled to the hearty congratulations showered upon them at the conclusion of hostilities.

RESULT: Bury 4 – Southampton 0

BURY: Thompson (goal); Darroch and Davidson (backs); Pray, Leeming and Ross (halves); Richards, Wood [1], McLuckie [2], Sagar and Plant [1] (forwards).
SOUTHAMPTON: Robinson (goal); Durber and Meehan (backs); Petrie, Chadwick and Meston (halves); Turner, Yates, Farrell, Wood and Milward (forwards).
Referee: Mr. A. Kingscott (Derby).

Attendance: 68945.

THE PRESENTATION

Former Prime Minister Lord Rosebery[15] had agreed to perform the presentation ceremony but when it had become clear that Bury were to be the victors he had insisted upon Lord James of Hereford, who was the president of the Bury club, taking over the honour.
London Evening Standard - Monday 23 April 1900

At the conclusion of the game there was a great rush to the front of the Pavilion. As the players entered the enclosure, Lord James of Hereford, the President of the Bury Club, came down the steps of the stand and shook hands warmly with Pray, the captain of the winning side. Mr. J. C. Clegg, the Chairman of the Council of the Football Association, then announced that Lord James would present the cup and medals, and that he had prevailed upon Lord Rosebery to say a few words to them subsequently.

---

15   Archibald Philip Primrose, 5th Earl of Rosebery, 1st Earl of Midlothian, KG, KT, PC, FRS, FBA

LORD JAMES OF HEREFORD said - Ladies and Gentlemen, this is a great honour I have had thrust upon me, of presenting the Cup to the winning Bury team. You feel, as I feel, that it is Lord Rosebery who ought to present the Cup, not myself, but we have been arguing the point for three-quarters of an hour, and it is he who has prevailed - as he would prevail in every other game against me - and he has induced me to take this duty. The superiority of my successful friend in every game entitles him to occupy this position. There is one game I see him playing elsewhere. He has a great following throughout the country, and in that game he always plays right forward, and I am afraid I am only a half-back (laughter). This is such a moving scene that I will only present this cup to my old friends from Bury, who have won it well, and they will do their best to defend it.

LORD JAMES.

Amid hearty cheering, LORD JAMES handed the cup to the Bury captain, for which Pray returned thanks, and asked the Bury players to give three hearty cheers for the losing team.

The cheers having been cordially given, Robinson came up to receive his medal, and LORD ROSEBERY moved forward and shook him warmly by the hand, saying, "I am glad to meet you again."

LORD JAMES OF HEREFORD (THE PRESIDENT OF THE BURY CLUB) PRESENTS THE CUP TO PRAY.

LORD ROSEBERY then said - "I have just asked one of the Bury players if he was not very tired, and his answer was, 'I am very dry' (laughter). Well, I am very dry too (renewed laughter) - more from a cold in my head than from any exertion in the football field, and therefore you will excuse me if I don't say much. We can all sing the praises of the Bury team to-day, and Lord James said a great deal about them. You will, however, allow me to drop one tear over Southampton. Might I mention one particular name? Twice in the last fortnight have I seen Mr. Robinson fight a gallant uphill fight against overwhelming odds, and I think we must all feel full of admiration for him to-day. I also feel admiration for Lord James, because it is a trying duty to present the cup before this large crowd, and I hope you will agree that a vote of thanks is due to him. This is the second year running you have had a distinguished Cabinet Minister amongst you to preside over this sport. It is good for football, and it is not bad for the Cabinet Minister (laughter). I move this, and it will be seconded by the Mayor of Southampton."

THE MAYOR OF SOUTHAMPTON seconded the Resolution, which was carried by acclamation.

After the match, the new Cup-holders quietly returned to their hotel at Covent Garden where they were to stay until returning to Bury on the Monday. The Cup travelled back to the hotel with them and was consecrated there in the customary fashion, captain Pray being the first, toasting his comrades with "Boys, Good Health!" Sunday was spent enjoying the gardens at Hampton Court before returning to a heroes welcome at Bury via the 2 p.m. Midland Express on Monday.

Manchester Courier - Tuesday 24 April 1900
THE ENGLISH CUP - WINNERS' RETURN.
BURY *EN FETE* - SPLENDID RECEPTION OF THE TEAM.
EXTRAORDINARY ENTHUSIASM.

The Bury football team returned home last evening from London, bringing with them that most coveted trophy the English Cup. Although not much to look at, being much less in size than the Lancashire Cup, the people who commented upon this fact must remember that it is not the size and value of the prize that are to be considered, but the honour attached to the winning of it. It is now nine years since Blackburn Rovers gained the distinction of holding the cup for a year by beating Everton at Preston, and each year since Lancashire teams have been living in hopes of once more bringing the Cup to the County Palatine. As everyone is aware, Bury vanquished Southampton at the Crystal Palace on Saturday, which enabled them to become the custodians of the cup for one year.

The successful team left St. Pancras at two o'clock yesterday afternoon and arrived at Victoria Station, Manchester, at a quarter to seven. The hour of their arrival having become known to the general public, there was an enormous concourse to witness the passing through Manchester of the victors. Number 6 platform, at which the London train drew up, was crowded with football enthusiasts, who greeted the Bury team with terrific cheering. Pray, the captain, came in for special recognition. He was overwhelmed with congratulations at the successful manner in which he had pioneered the Bury Eleven. The other members of the team also came in for much hand-shaking, and it was with the greatest of difficulty that the saloon containing the "Shakers" was shunted alongside No. 7 platform, where it was attached to a special train for Bury. The special, it need hardly be said, was literally packed, and all available standing room was taken up. Manchester was left amidst the explosion of a score of fog-signals and the prolonged cheering of the multitude. At the intermediate stations the team and its supporters were speedily recognised and vociferously greeted. At Whitefield the famous Besses-o'-the-Barn prize band entrained, having voluntarily offered their services to escort the team to their headquarters, the Queen's Hotel, Bury.

Bury, like other towns, has had its many opportunities to display enthusiasm, such as the Jubilee, the Diamond jubilee, and set-offs to the war, but it is safe to assert that last night's demonstration far surpassed any previous occasion. Lancashire people are thorough lovers of sporting, and if the inhabitants of Bury never before realised the value of their football team, they made up for lost time last night, and gave honour where honour was due, by cheering them to the echo. The arrival at Bolton-street Station Bury, was accompanied by a scene unparalleled in the history of the town. The station and its approaches for several hundred yards were crowded with thousands of people of both sexes, who had taken up their positions for some hours in order to give their champions the royal welcome which they so richly merited. Councillor Byron (the Mayor of Bury) and several of his colleagues were present to receive the team. As Pray emerged from the saloon holding aloft the English Cup it was the signal for a great outburst of cheering, which was kept up for several minutes. The Mayor gave them a hearty welcome, speaking of various things the borough was noted for, and referred to the fact that it had been instrumental in producing Vardon, the champion golfer of the world.

Outside the station the team and officials entered three waggonettes, but the greatest difficulty was experienced in starting on a procession round the town. But the Bury police force controlled the crowd in an admirable manner, and the wonder is that someone was not injured, there being many narrow escapes. The route taken was along Bolton-street, Silver-street, Haymarket-street, down to Elton-street, and back to the Queen's Hotel, the team's headquarters. The streets were lined by thousands of people, and when it is considered that each particular person, large or small, short or tall, was imbued with the utmost enthusiasm and anxious to give vent to it, some idea may be gathered of the remarkable demonstration. The Parish Churchyard wall was utilised by crowds of people, and even the most dangerous points of vantage were occupied to give the victorious "Shakers" a passing cheer.

The scene in front of the Queen's Hotel baffles all description, and the sight awakened wonderment as to where all the people came from. The thousands of upturned joyous faces, made a most imposing spectacle - one which will live long in the memories of all who witnessed it. The cheering was loud and prolonged, and the band could not be heard more than a few yards away. Arrived in their room at the hotel, the crowd in the street commenced to shout for Plant, who, after much persuasion, said in his usual brusque manner, "Aw'll just give 'em a smile!" He did, and the applause was deafening. Alderman Brierley occupied the chair at a subsequent gathering, and said that every man went into the field on Saturday afternoon purposing to do his duty, and he did it. Pray said he was highly honoured by being the captain of the Bury team. Mr. Albert Duckworth paid tribute to the high standard of behaviour of the Bury players. Festivities of all descriptions were the order until a late hour, and few who were present will ever forget the advent of the English Cup into Bury.

Bury's share of the Cup Final 'gate' amounted to £938 16s. 6d. with a further £350 1s. 6d. accruing from the semi finals. This completed a remarkable financial turnaround for the club, reversing a negative balance of around £1,200 at the start of the season into a positive one of a similar amount by it's end!

THE REDS HAVE IT.

THE BURY LEFT WING FORWARD GETS BALL AND SHOOTS TO ROBINSON WITHOUT SCORING.

F.A. Cup Winners - 1900

In Picture (players Only):
Elevated: Darroch, Montgomery (reserve), Thompson, Davidson
Standing: Pray, Leeming, Ross / **Seated:** Wood, McLuckie, Sagar / **On Ground:** Richards, Plant

The Between Years

1900/01
1st Round (09/02/1901)
The Wednesday 0-1 **Bury**
2nd Round (23/02/1901)
Tottenham Hotspur 2-1 **Bury**

1901/02
1st Round (25/01/1902)
Bury 5-1 West Bromwich Albion
2nd Round (08/02/1902)
Walsall 0-5 **Bury**
3rd Round (22/02/1902)
Bury 2-3 Southampton

Bury's first defence of the trophy began on familiar ground, or rather the familiarly unfamiliar, with yet another away draw, against The Wednesday at Sheffield (Hillsborough). The next round took them on their travels again, this time to London to take on Tottenham Hotspur who, like last season's beaten finalists, Southampton, were then member's of the Southern League. That was where Bury's defence of the cup ended, as the 'Spurs recorded a 2-1 victory before going on to achieve what the Southampton club the previous year could not, becoming the first (and last) Southern League club ever to lift the trophy. Since then no club outside of the top two tiers of League football (including more latterly the Premier League) has ever done so.

The following season, Bury began their involvement in the Cup tourney with a home draw against West Bromwich Albion - which must have seemed something of a novelty to the Gigg-laners who had not received a home tie since the visit of Stoke in the first round four years previously. Since then, in seven successive rounds over three consecutive seasons (not counting the Final and Semi-Final ties played on neutral grounds) they had been drawn away from home on every occasion. After disposing of West Bromwich they repeated the feat against Walsall in the second round before a return encounter with Southampton in the third. On that occasion, Southampton gained their revenge for the Cup Final defeat of two seasons previous in winning by the odd goal in five in a thriller at Gigg-lane. The Buryites, however, had the consolation of having carried the County Palatine flag further than any other Lancashire club in the competition that season. Southampton went on to reach the final again, but again failed at the final hurdle, beaten by Sheffield United after a replay.

In Bury's Cup winning season the club finished their League Division One campaign in 12th place (out of 18). The following season they improved that finish to 5th, the club's best finish to that point (and not to be improved until the 1925/26 season when the club finished 4th). The club's accounts that season showed another substantial profit of £438 11s. 10. The season after Bury finished 7th in the First Division, and recorded a profit on that term of £36 19s. 2d.

The 1902/03 season began with Bury among the early front runners. Indeed by mid-October Bury were second in the table by just one point from Sheffield United but with no fewer than three games in hand! Unfortunately, a string of injuries then followed which told heavily on Bury's small squad so that they began to slip down the table. Chief among the injured was Charles Sagar who dislocated his shoulder so badly whilst playing for the English League in the inter-League match against Ireland at Belfast that his services were lost to the club for six weeks. This led to a conflict between the Bury club and the League executive when the latter refused to accept any responsibility for the player's injury and declined Bury's request to contribute towards his wages during his period of inaction. Since the inter-League matches provided a major source of income for the League authorities, who did not pay their respective clubs for the services of those players that made that income possible, the Bury directors had felt it only fair that they should be compensated for the loss to the club occasioned by that service. Consequently the Bury directors gave notice of their intention to file a motion at the next League A.G.M. for the abolition of inter-League matches. This would have meant raising the clubs annual subscriptions to cover the shortfall in income but might still have found backing from other clubs who had experienced Bury's situation. The Next League A.G.M. however, was still several months away, being not due till the end of the season on 2th May, 1903.

1902/03 - The First Round

Bury started their 1902/03 Cup campaign with a home tie against the Wolverhampton Wanderers, the first ever meeting of the two sides in Cup competition. Based upon recent League results Bury were the in form side, but it has always been the case that Cup performances have little to do with League form! Both sides were taking the tie very seriously and had been preparing for the event by training in the bracing sea air of the Lancashire coast, the Wolves at Southport and Bury at Lytham.

Among the other ties Derby County faced Small Heath[16] at the Baseball Ground. Derby were, at the time, the bridesmaids (never the bride!) of the F.A. cup, having reached the semi-final stage no fewer than five times in the previous seven seasons, twice going on to contest the final but losing on both occasions. The Heathens, in contrast, had never advanced beyond the third round proper, and had only reached that stage of the competition on a single occasion. Indeed, more often than not in their prior history in the competition they had gone out at the first time of asking.

BURY v. WOLVERHAMPTON WANDERERS
at Gigg Lane, Bury – Saturday 7th February, 1903
Athletic News - Monday 09 February 1903
Bury's Lucky Win [By Sprinter]

Rain, which fell heavily on Friday night and continued its merciless downpour right up to the moment Mr. A.G. Hines's whistle denoted the start of the tie at Bury, frightened away two-thirds of the usual crowd that attends the arena at Gigg-lane, and when the home eleven and Wolverhampton Wanderers lined up there were little more than 5000 people present. The ground, despite the rain, was in beautiful condition, and it is wonderful how well the turf wears at Bury. The Wolves had the same side out that split points with West Bromwich Albion last week, with the exception that Beats at outside right took Bowens place. Neither Gray nor Wood figured in the Bury front rank, Berry partnering Plant, while little Lamberton helped Richards. Incidents during the course of the game crowded themselves one upon the other. There never was a dull instant, and it was anybody's game until well after the interval.

Bury, winning the toss, decided to play with the hurricane at their backs, and in the first moment Plant took a corner and Frank Thorpe gave Baddeley his first handful. Then Plant, on the run, treated him likewise, and a second later Thorpe, gathering the ball in a masterly manner from Plant's pass, caused Baddeley once more to use his brains as well as his hands. This great pressure upon the visiting defenders held out hopes to the home spectatorate, but Jones and Betteley were in glorious form, and Baddeley as cool as a cucumber. In a flash, in consequence of some poor tackling by the home backs, Smith got going and brought Monteith down on to his face. The goalkeeper seemed utterly lost for the second, but he recovered wonderfully, and flung the sphere away, to the accompaniment of a big "Oh" from the grandstand. The next moment

---

16 Now Birmingham City.

Baddeley fumbled the ball in a similar manner but got it away it despite the attentions of Lamberton, whose one aim all through the game was to go for the goalkeeper - a policy that did not come off, and caused much grumbling among the keen judges of the game, and which certainly lost his side a goal on one occasion. Picking out some of the many incidents of the initial half, it will be as well to mention Plant's striking the upright with a fine flying shot; Wooldridge's over anxiety, which lost him a goal when Monteith had miskicked; Frank Thorpe's pot shot from an awkward angle, which dropped on the bar in front of Baddeley; and Beats' series of tussles with McEwen, which did not redound to the credit of either, for they were both "doing a little bit." But all and every effort came to nought, and at half-time the score sheet was blank.

The goal that decided the match - for Bury - came 15 minutes or so after the adjournment. It was remarkable that Bury had failed with the wind behind them – be it said it was really astonishing how they once or twice escaped, for their backs were poor compared with Jones and Betteley, and frequently let the Wanderers in - yet in the second half, playing with the big breeze in their teeth, the "Shakers" were at times all over the "Wolves'," and early on Sagar, who caught up one of the very few "middles" that came his way on the end of his toe shot just outside, the ball rattling the stick which supports the net. Hereabouts Sagar was constantly bobbing up and down, and Richards, too, who seemed to have wakened up from a period of sleep, got going gaily. At this period of the game also the Wanderers resorted to some little tricks which might be called "shady" by Eugene Stratton[17], and although in some places they received their *quid pro quo*, the fault was mainly on the shoulders of the visitors. Sagar, despite the attentions of Walker - who is not a nice man to ruffle the temper of - once treated us to a little passing *tete-a-tete* with Richards, and as the outcome of it Bury got their winning goal. The ball was in the vicinity of Baddeley's charge, and Sagar, finding he could do nothing with it, slipped it across to **Richards**. He hesitated a moment, the chance looked lost, but gathering himself together, the light haired youth landed the ball into the net at the top hand corner and out of Baddeley's reach. I think the first intimation that Richards had that he had done something big was when his arm was nearly shaken off by his jubilant companions, and then, pale with the excitement of the moment, he took his place for the centre kick. The goal had a bad effect upon the Wanderers, for although up to this period, as I have said, it was anyone's game, they were now a beaten side, and Bury should have had another goal, if not two. Sagar once made Baddeley fly up in the air to save a great shot, and except for an occasional break away by Miller Bury finished up the game in a distinctly aggressive mood.

Cup tie football is notable for a certain thing, and we get plenty of it at Gigg-lane. It was the only blur on a great match. There were three pairs of foemen who were constantly breaking the laws, and I felt sorry that Charles Sagar should receive as much undue attention. He was victimised more than anybody. There were two very weak spots in the Bury armour, and it was surprising to note how badly Thorpe played. He gave an exhibition altogether below his usual standard, and shaped at times like a mere novice. Lamberton persisted in playing the man instead of the ball, and sometimes utterly neglected Richards, who, as the end drew nigh, allowed the little man to do what he pleased. As a forward line the Bury five were just the superior of their opponents, although Lamberton and Berry were not to be thoroughly relied upon. Plant hardly

---

17 Eugene Stratton – American born blackface dancer popular in British music halls.

touched the ball in the second half, so much work did Sagar and Richards do, aided by Lamberton, whose zeal was rather misplaced. Plant, however, did finely in the first half, and one of his shots deserved a goal. With their regular front rank, Bury should advance a few stages in the cup, and, while he is in his present form, Leeming is a better man than Thorpe. Johnston and Ross were ever to the fore, and the cunning play of the last named was at times really remarkable. Lindsay and McEwen played by no means up to their reputations, but Montieth did all that was required of him. On behalf of the Wanderers Beats persevered manfully as did the other outside man, Miller, who had an able Lieutenant in Wooldridge; but Smith and Heywood did not shine with any amount of brilliance. The half-backs were a worrying trio, not over scrupulous, but theirs was useful work indeed. Betteley and Jones were far ahead of their opposing pair of backs, Lindsay and McEwen, but Baddeley hardly knew what was going to be done with the ball that beat him, and in consequence of the indecision on the part of Sagar and Richards, the goalkeeper paid the penalty. Really, it was a lucky goal, for it came off when everyone seemed at his wit's end what to do with the ball, but it gave Bury their entry into the second round.

RESULT: Bury 1 – Wolverhampton Wanderers 0

BURY: Monteith (goal); Lindsay and McEwen (backs); Johnston, Thorpe and Ross (halves); Richards [1], Lamberton, Sagar, Berry and Plant (forwards).
WOLVERHAMPTON: Baddeley (goal); Betteley and Jones (backs); Annis, Walker and Whitehouse (halves); Miller, Wooldridge, Smith, Haywood and Beats (forwards).
Referee: A.G. Hines (Nottingham).

DERBY COUNTY v. SMALL HEATH[18]
The Baseball Ground, Derby – Saturday 7th February, 1903
Athletic News - Monday 09 February 1903
Derby County Win a Capital Match [By Peakite]

Derby County have no particular fault to find in the weather they have had this season. On several important occasions it has obliged them in the most remarkable manner, and Saturday proved no exception to the rule. There was a high wind blowing, but appearances were strongly suggestive of rain if the breeze should chance to moderate. However, it kept off, and the Baseball ground presented a crowded appearance in the popular parts, there being quite 15,000 spectators in attendance. The higher priced portions of the pavilion, however, were almost deserted, and it is certain that the clubs would have increased their aggregate receipts had they been content with a more moderate charge. The composition of the Derby team did not inspire a vast amount of confidence, as Goodall and Leckie were both absentees, the former suffering from a boil on his thigh, while the latter had not recovered from the shaking his weak knee received in the Bury match. The half-back line was therefore completed by the inclusion of Lloyd and May, while John Boag made his second appearance of the season at centre forward in a match of any importance. On the Small Heath side Wharton was unable to play, but Leonard turned out with his finger in splints. There

---

18   Now Birmingham City.

was joy in the county camp when Bloomer won the toss and secured the advantage of the wind for the first half of the game.

It was blowing right down the ground towards the Town goal, and great as was the assistance it afforded the home team at starting, it was also a source of embarrassment to their forwards who were a long time ere they could accommodate themselves to the pace at which the ball travels. Robinson, however, saved twice from Richards, whilst Boag, who was putting in a lot of fine work in the centre just missed the mark more than once. Small Heath made several business like incursions into Derby Territory, and once after Morris had been penalised for a foul on Athersmith the ball was dropped in threatening fashion in front of Fryer, but a claim for off-side brought relief. The style in which the county were playing with the wind in their favour was not very hopeful, but Robinson had once saved finely from Richards, and had two narrow escapes of being charged through his own goal. From a corner kick well placed by Warrington the ball passed into the net without a second player touching it, whilst Morris skimmed the crossbar with a beautiful long shot. In this way we got within measurable distance of half-time, but just as the Small Heath supporters were pluming themselves on the certainty of a clean sheet the alluring prospect was dashed from their lips. John May, at 25 yards range, had sent in a fast low shot that Robinson only half saved, and **Boag**, lying handy, met the ball on the rebound and banged it into the net. Altogether a capital goal and well earned.

If Derby County had not done everything that had been expected of them in the first half, no fault can be found in the character of their subsequent display. Their forwards did much more effective work against the wind than they had done with it, and Boag's policy of banging the ball out to his wings was completely successful. They repeatedly carried the war into the enemies camp, and Richards with a couple of fine passes placed the Small Heath goal in extreme jeopardy. So well did the county play that the confidence of their supporters was soon restored, and halfway through this half **Warrington** clinched matters by scoring a capital goal from a corner kick. Small Heath afterwards had more of the game, and Fryer handled several good shots from Leonard ere he was eventually beaten from a corner kick by **Windridge**. This was 10 minutes from the close, but the effort came too late, as the county defence never gave their opponents an opportunity of equalising and Derby won fairly and squarely by two goals to one.

It struck me that the match was interesting above the general run of cup ties. There was a lot of excellent forward work on both sides, and the way each in turn struggled to overcome the difficulties created by the wind was really fine. On the whole, Derby played the better game, and deserved their victory. Boag led their forwards on in his best style, and showed once more that he is the best man for the position the County have, especially for cup tie work. Warrington was perhaps the weakest of the forwards, but it must be remembered that he scored a fine goal and made some useful passes. The left wing displayed some of its old cleverness, and was stronger than the right. Lloyd, though by no means an Archie Goodall, played a good winning game, and Warren enjoyed himself as much as ever in games of this class. He's really a wonderful cup tie player, and challenged comparison with Charles Morris, at full-back. The small Heath players were not far short of being as clever as their opponents in attack,

Leonard shooting at goal with great persistency. Their defence, however, was by no means as steady, and that was where they lost the game.

RESULT: Derby County 2 – Small Heath 1

DERBY CO.: Fryer (goal); Methven and Morris (backs); Warren, Lloyd and May (halves); Warrington [1], Bloomer, Boag [1], Richards and Davis (forwards).
SMALL HEATH: Robinson (goal); Goldie and Wassell (backs); Jones, Wigmore and Dougherty (halves); Athersmith, Leonard, McRoberts, Windridge [1] and Field (forwards).
Referee: Mr. N. Whittaker (London).

OTHER RESULTS

7th February 1903

Aston Villa	4–1	Sunderland
Barnsley	2–0	Lincoln City
Blackburn Rovers	0–0	The Wednesday
Bolton Wanderers	0–5	Bristol City
Everton	5–0	Portsmouth
Glossop	2–3	Stoke
Grimsby Town	2–1	Newcastle United
Millwall Athletic	3–0	Luton Town
Newton Heath	2-1	Liverpool
Notts County	0–0	Southampton
Nottingham Forest	0–0	Reading
Preston North End	3–1	Manchester City
Tottenham Hotspur	0–0	West Bromwich Albion
Woolwich Arsenal	1–3	Sheffield United

11th February 1903

Southampton	2–2	Notts County
West Bromwich Albion	0–2	Tottenham Hotspur

12th February 1903

Reading	3–6	Nottingham Forest
The Wednesday	0–1	Blackburn Rovers

16th February 1903

Notts County	2–1	Southampton

1902/1903 - The Second Round

The second round saw Bury travelling to Bramall Lane to antagonise Sheffield United in a replay of the semi-final tie of their cup winning year. Sheffield United had been the current Cup holders on that occasion, and, by a strange quirk of coincidence, were the holders again on this occasion – an omen, perhaps, that if Bury were to defeat them they might again go on to take their place. Sheffield had to face Bury without Alf Common and Ernest Needham, two of their key players and two of the most famous names of their era. Over the previous five seasons, however, the Blades had reached three F.A. Cup finals, capturing the trophy twice and playing no fewer than 34 Cup ties in the process. In this run they had on several occasions shown a disregard for bad luck and a contempt for adversity in the face of absences of key players that was truly worthy of great Cup fighting sides.

Derby's second round opponents were Blackburn Rovers, and the two sides had met in a rehearsal of the tie, playing out their English League fixture, at the same venue exactly one week previously. Derby had won that game by virtue of a late penalty. Blackburn at the time, in League terms, were mired low in the table and embroiled in the struggle to avoid relegation. For the match, Derby were able to rely on their full first eleven, whilst Blackburn were without namesake Fred Blackburn, their exciting England International flying winger. The Lancastrians, however, were legendary cup fighters, so whilst the form books may have predicted a Derby victory, nothing could be taken for granted.

On the day, virtually the whole of the country was wracked by gale-force winds which in some areas combined with snow storms to create blizzard-like conditions, so that it was remarkable that all eight games in the Cup competition were played in full, although several were subjected to lengthy interruptions whilst the worst of the weather abated.

SHEFFIELD UNITED V. BURY
at Bramall Lane, Sheffield – Saturday 21st February, 1903
Athletic News - Monday 23 February 1903
Bury beat the cup holders [By Tittyrus]

Atrocious is the only adjective which adequately describes the conditions prevailing at Bramall-lane on Saturday, for it seemed as if after a Spring-like week all nature had conspired to spoil the match as an exhibition of science and as a spectacle. Half a hurricane howled over the crow's nest devoted to the Press at Bramall-lane, and the rain was driven along by the breeze with such forces and fury that even a National cup tie had to suffer interruption. Footballers are not featherbed sportsmen, but the ten minutes cessation of hostilities was quite justified. Never did cricketers scamper for the pavilion with greater zest than these players. But that ten minutes which had been devoted to the game had sufficed to give Bury a lead which they retained to the end. The ground was a sea of mud, and served to remind our artist of the match at Carolina Port when Dundee played Glasgow Rangers, and the coin with which the captains tossed for choice of goals was buried in the mud. So deeply was it embedded that the crowd laughed while it was dug out. After the storm which caused the stoppage Bramall-lane was dotted with miniature lakes, and the players were interesting studies in black and white, but chiefly black. Players missed their kicks, lost their foothold on the treacherous turf, and, as a rule, a charge resulted in both men alighting on Mother Earth, and sliding a few yards on their south-western extremities. But the patience of the people, especially those out in the open, was astounding, and recalled to mind the remark of the famous Roman general, who asserted that his legions had slept in the open air for fourteen years. The modern football enthusiast is endowed with a hardihood of this description. Despite the dreadful conditions the players battled nobly, and Bury had the satisfaction of vanquishing the cup holders by 1-0, just the same as two years ago the Gigg lane eleven hied them to Owlerton, and dismissed Sheffield Wednesday by exactly the same score. But I am firmly of opinion that Bury ought on Saturday to have prevailed by a considerably wider margin.

Bury, who had to face the wind and the rain, went off at such a pace that Boyle, from an extraordinarily acute angle, kicked the ball through his own goal, to the consternation of Lewis, but fortunately for the United the whistle had already been sounded for offside against Leeming. But Sagar was the man of the moment, and after he had caused Lewis to kick out, the Bury centre scored an exceedingly clever goal. There was a long lobbing return from the half-back line. I think the ball came from Ross, and was descending within about half a dozen yards of goal. Boyle was on the lookout, but **Sagar**, who is quite an artist at hooking and heeling, shot out his foot rearwards and with his heel brought the ball over his own head, and then dashing in applied his cranium to the ball and placed it snugly in the leather at the moment Lewis grassed him near the post, and his own comrades rushed up to lift him out of the mire and wring his hand. Thus was the winning point notched at the end of 5 minutes. Very shortly after, play was suspended for ten minutes, at what time shelter was most comforting. But on restarting the United kept up a splendid sustained attack, in which the ball never rested, so incessantly was it kept on the move. The point of danger was constantly changed, and in these operations Bennett, Chapman, and Johnson were very prominent, but Lindsay, Ross, and McEwen were resolute and reliable in defence. Bennett was the man whose centres boded danger, and Bennett was the man who ended the sustained excitement by shooting a foot outside the netted haven. From the goal kick Thicket made a long return which bounced in front of Monteith, and would have entered the goal over the custodians head had he not adroitly turned the ball over the bar. But this, and all other corner kicks were unproductive, and Bury began to assert themselves once more. Leeming and Sagar repeatedly passed out to Plant, who made swinging shots towards goal, leaving the other forwards to rush ahead. This was a more paying policy than the short inside game which the United tried, for the ball would not travel in the mud. Still, whenever Bennett got the leather he made fine centres, but Monteith never failed to anticipate trouble and remove it. From one of their left wing dashes Bury were conceded a corner, which Richards placed nicely. Leeming headed the ball to Plant, who found the net with a brilliant shot. I thought this a good and a clever goal, and was much astonished when Mr. Millward annulled it, and gave a free kick yards away from Plant for impeding the goalkeeper. I could not see the justice of this ruling, but the referee's supremacy must be upheld. Wilkinson took up the story and transferred to Bennett, who made yet another grand centre, which Monteith diverted, but only for Priest to head just over the bar. Still priest was not the only man who failed, for Sagar, Leeming, and Wood were in turn all in excellent scoring positions, and did not profit at the golden moment. It would not have been surprising had Bury been three goals up instead of one at the interval, but, on the other hand, there is no denying that Sheffield were very plucky and persevering, and that Monteith alone kept them at bay by his astute goalkeeping.

In the second portion of play the game considerably deteriorated, for it was more of a severe scramble than concerted movement and combination. Again had Monteith more work than Lewis, and it was astonishing how the Bury goalkeeper saved the situation once when there was a misunderstanding between him and Lindsay. In a loose scrimmage the players were piled one on the other until the referee intervened and decided to throw up the ball. There was then another mighty struggle, but Parker unfortunately handled, and so brought relief to Bury, who resisted many other onslaughts, and eventually ran out the winners by the bare goal.

The game was a desperate struggle, and considering the conditions, good to watch. It must not be forgotten that Bury would have preferred a fast and dry ground, and to win under such circumstances is to their infinite credit. Thrice was the ball in the United goal, but only once was a valid point allowed, though I never saw a sounder goal than that which Plant secured. But Sagar, who won the match, had one opportunity of scoring when he had no one to beat save Lewis, and his final effort was almost a random shot. Yet on another occasion Leeming should have netted - and these are facts which tend to prove that Bury deserved their victory, although their forward line, as a whole, was not so clever as that of United. Still the defence of the victors commanded the admiration of everybody. They withstood sustained attack after attack most manfully. It may be urged that the United experienced hard luck but on the other hand they never outwitted the defence, they never urged the ball into the net during the game, and so in my view the Lancastrian's deserved their victory and all the spoils attaching to it. Bury owe their success primarily to Sagar's artistry, but quite as much to the vigilance and ability of Monteith, and to the resourcefulness and reliability of Lindsay at back. Of course all share in the Glory of such a memorable win, but this trio are entitled to more than ordinary commendation. Sagar, despite occasional mistakes, was a great factor in opening out of the game and a source of danger near goal, but he deteriorated as the tie grew older. But Monteith was always consistent. He might have been rather slow in disposing of the ball sometimes, and so courted difficulties with his opponents, but he never allowed any ball to pass him, and in two duels with forwards swarming all over him he still came out invincible. No one did more to win the tie. Lindsey's returns were a feature of the match, and nine times out of ten he met the greasy heavy ball with his instep, and was thus always safe in his method. Moreover his judgement was almost unfailing, so that he rarely missed being in the right place, and he was quite the master of Lipsham. McEwen was useful, and the same may be said of all the Bury half backs, of whom Frank Thorpe was often conspicuous as a despoiler of combination and a provider of of opportunities for his own forwards. The Bury attackers are not so formidable as of yore, for Richards and Wood have lost some of their powers, but Leeming's passes were usually admirable. Plant never lacked opportunity, but he was erratic and did not always play or centre so accurately as he should have done. But if the Bury vanguard did not show the fine art of football they adapted themselves to the mudlarking, and they swung the ball about by long passes, which on such a day were very disconcerting to their antagonists, who were often puzzled and tired by this changing in the point of attack. The cup holders were in no wise overplayed; on the contrary, they had, as they phrase runs, much more of the play than the visitors; but there was not quite that devil in front of goal we have seen the United display. Their shooting, although often on the target, and with some sting in the ball, was not of that penetrating character which causes a goalkeeper to look on in sheer dismay. Still, the United forwards were a busy body, but they tried to do too much combination, and would have been advised to revert to the old plan of kick, rush, and shoot. Bennett was unquestionably the most dangerous wing man on the field. Rarely did he make a centre which went behind the goal line - and he put the ball in many times, but I thought he might have been more incisive when he came in for close quarter work. Hedley showed good command of the ball, and played a very serviceable game, but Chapman, Priest, and Lipsham never rose above mediocrity. I liked the Sheffield half backs, and although all of them are excellent, Johnson revelled in the heavy going, and was prodigious as an obstructionist. Some of his centres, too, rivalled those of Bennett. At back Boyle is entitled to share the honours with Lindsay, and it would be impossible to praise his value too highly. Lewis had a light task compared with Monteith.

RESULT: Sheffield United 0 – Bury 1

BURY: Monteith (goal); Lindsay and McEwen (backs); Johnston, Thorpe and Ross (halves); Richards, Lamberton, Sagar [1], Leeming and Plant (forwards).

SHEFFIELD UTD: Lewis (goal); Thickett and Boyle (backs); Johnson, Morren and Wilkinson (halves); Bennett, Chapman, Hedley, Priest and Lipsham (forwards).
Referee: Mr. A. Millward (London).

DERBY COUNTY v. BLACKBURN ROVERS
at the Baseball Ground, Derby – Saturday 21st February, 1903

Sporting Life - Monday 23 February 1903
DERBY MAINTAIN LEAGUE FORM

The curtain raiser which these teams had at the Baseball Ground a week ago last Saturday seemed to increase the interest in the Cup tie on Saturday. The Rovers lost the League game by a penalty goal in the last few minutes of the game and felt very sore about it. Still, they fancied they could win the Cup tie, and they and some 4,000 supporters appeared at the Peak capital in confident humour. They had not spent a lot of money on training; they had gone on long walks in the country, had vegetated on Blackpool promenade for a few hours, and altogether felt able to beat creation. The Derby men, too, had done preparation at home, and though they did not feel quite so perky, if one might judge by their manner, still they felt quietly confident in touching Round Three. They had Archie Goodall back in their half-back ranks, and their team was at full strength. The Rovers, on the other hand, dropped out Blackburn, their left wing International, and played Swarbrick, while Dewhurst went among the half backs, where he has often played well this winter. The ground was not in bad order, and all that detracted from a perfect afternoon was that the wind was too high. It blew from goal to goal, and the Rovers had to face it in the first moiety.

Right off the County came away, and after contesting every inch of the ground, Davis whipped off to Boag, who headed forward, the ball wide before Warrington could reach it. Bloomer immediately afterwords sent behind, and the Rovers forced the play. Watson compelled Fryer to handle. Aided by the wind, the County men were soon at the other end, where Morris took a rash shot at thirty yards range. The Rovers played up, and the Derby citadel almost fell. Monks landed the ball into the goalmouth, only for it to be instantly punted back. McClure, with a deft shot, returned, but the defence prevailed. The Black and Whites raced forth *en masse*, and after much finessing on the part of the Rovers a corner was forced, and the ball was lifted clean into a ruck of players. After a short scrimmage the ball dropped at the feet of **Bloomer**. Like lightning, the latter player made no mistake, but placed the ball at the back of McIver in the rigging. This was only twelve minutes after the beginning, the Derby players and spectators were downright pleased. The home lot had a bit the best of matters after this. The strong wind prevented the players from anything like controlling the ball, and some shots were fearfully erratic. Swarbrick was winded by a heavy charge by Warren in an assault on the County goal. Richards drove over the crossbar, and McClure a few minutes later made a wonderful clearance. Whittaker sped away along the touch-line and whipped across a clever centre. Methven was extremely agile, and set his forwards going. Morris gave the Blue and Whites a corner, but owing to the wind the kick was a poor one. Eastham miskicked, and Boag lost a golden opportunity. Four corners were forced off the Rovers in less than two minutes just before the interval, but their defence was just perfect. Half-time score: Derby County, one goal; Rovers, nil.

In the second half the rain fell in much heavier fashion, and the ground became soft and muddy. The Derby men, though they were now facing the wind, played well. A magnificent sole effort by Davis almost brought disaster, but the backs were quick and sure. Crompton lifted the ball to his forwards, and just as Watson was going to take the pass Methven nipped in, and sent the ball flying up the field. Boag got the better of McClure after a hard struggle, and before Crompton could get to him Boag shot wide. A brilliant sprint by Davis ended by him shooting. The ball rebounded from the foot of Eastham to Boag again, who immediately tipped towards McIver. The ball, however, want to the foot of **Warrington**, who banged the sphere into the rigging behind McIver. The second goal put a damper on the enthusiasm of the Blackburn supporters. The Rovers rallied, and Watson fed Swarbrick. He drove across, but Methven and Morris were safe. McIver was compelled to leave his charge in order to beat Warrington. In the race for the ball the little Blue and White proved victorious, and the Rovers saved. The Derby men were now apparently content with their position. The Rovers worked manfully, but they found the home defence downright safe and good. The play continued interesting right up to the sounding of the whistle, when Derby won by:

RESULT: Derby County 2 – Blackburn Rovers 0

DERBY COUNTY: Fryer (goal); Methven and Morris (backs); Warren, Goodall and May (halves); Warrington [1], Bloomer [1], Boag, Richards and Davis (forwards).
BLACKBURN ROVERS: McIver (goal); Crompton and Eastham (backs); Dewhurst, McClure and Robertson (halves); Whittaker, Monks, Watson, Bow and Swarbrick (forwards).
Referee: Mr. A.J. Barker (Hanley).

OTHER RESULTS

21 February 1903

Nottingham Forest	0–0	Stoke
Aston Villa	4–1	Barnsley
Grimsby Town	0–2	Notts County
Derby County	2–0	Blackburn Rovers
Everton	3–1	Manchester United
Sheffield United	0–1	Bury
Millwall Athletic	4–1	Preston North End
Tottenham Hotspur	1–0	Bristol City

26 February 1903

Stoke	2–0	Nottingham Forest

1902/1903 - The Third Round

The third round saw Bury gain a home draw against Notts. County whilst Derby County entertained Stoke.

Even though they trailed Bury by a considerable margin in the League competition, County were the pundits choice for victory at Gigg Lane due to having done most of their best work that season away from home and a reputation of reserving their best form for the Cup competition.

Derby and Stoke each had injury concerns over key men prior to their encounter, both doubtful through knee injuries. For Derby, Steve Bloomer, was one of the most formidable and free-scoring forwards in the country, best known for his cannonball daisy cutters (ground level shots hit with tremendous power). For Stoke Leigh Richmond Roose was their Welsh International goalkeeper and one of the increasingly few remaining amateurs in the game still playing at the highest levels. His better than 1:4 record of clean sheets for Stoke (no goals against in 1 of every 4 matches played) was all the more remarkable given that his club were struggling against relegation most of his time with them. The doubts over the pair robbed the tie of what would otherwise have been the mouth-watering prospect of a duel of irresistible force meeting immoveable object. Influential as Bloomer was, however, his fellow forwards had a reputation of playing up in his absence, so that Stoke's loss was by far the greater.

Again, the contest was plagued by bad weather, with high winds being experienced at all four centres where ties were contested, though the accompanying rains were much lighter than on the occasion of the previous round.

BURY v. NOTTS COUNTY
at Gigg Lane, Bury – 7th March, 1903
Sporting Life - Monday 9th March, 1903
BURY v. NOTTS COUNTY

{Warning – as a historical record the following report is reproduced verbatim but contains a word and an allusion that may now be considered racially offensive.}

The game between these teams in the third round of the English Cup competition was played on the Bury enclosure on Saturday, before a gate of some 20,000 people, the amount realised being £870. When the draw was first made known it was by general consent agreed that these teams would play one of the hardest games of the four, and so it proved. The teams had each undergone preparations for the game. The Notts men had been at their pleasant quarters at Hazleford on the Trent, doing mild but serviceable work, while the Bury players had been keeping themselves in condition on the banks of the River Ribble at Lytham. The Notts team only left Nottingham on Saturday morning, and arrived at the South Lancashire town about noon. The home players too, adopted a similar course, driving up not long before they were due to play. The morning had been bad, hail and cold rain showers had alternated with dashes of cold winter sunshine, and the whole was rendered more uncomfortable by a nasty north-west wind.

The Notts men were the first off to serious work, and amid a silence which told of fear for the safety of the Bury headquarters, W. Ross sent in a dangerous shot, which nearly brought disaster. It was a narrow escape. Wood dashed away to the other end in promising style, and a corner was won by Richards, from which Leeming sent very close. Notts again made the pace with spirit, but Johnston brought relief, and the home right attacked in a fashion raising strong hopes. Richards, though very closely pressed by Montgomery, got in a fine shot again. The Shakers bore down in earnest fashion, Sagar leading the van, and passing out to Plant, whose centre brought a couple of corners, splendidly placed by Richards, and from the second of which Johnston drove a few inches over a nasty dropping shot. Despite the wind Bury were the better side, and pressed with grand purpose. Twice Sagar and his left wing ran along swiftly, and once Plant fired one of his cannon balls, which was not far off the target. The determined home players secured another corner, and it was, indeed, lucky for Notts that a tremendous shot by Thorpe cannoned off one of their players. Then, again, before Notts could get clear, Proud sent behind from a few yards range, an almost impossible performance. Notts failed to make much impression on the home defence, though Whyte several times got in good little runs and centres which were not turned to account. The teams appeared a bit afraid of each other. The Shakers were showing very little in the way of attack, and their supporters called on them, "Play up. Bury." By and by there was a revival among the Shakers forwards, and loud applause greeted a sustained effort, finished by Sagar shooting over. Richards, on the right, was by no means so fast and clever as usual, and Montgomery, playing against him, had a tendency to unfairness. Thorpe twice won applause for returns, in which his long reach figured prominently. From a free kick against Wood there was a tussle in the home goal mouth, and Bull collided violently with Sagar, who received a severe shaking. On resuming, Ross spoiled Whyte, but Green got in a shot which curled in obliquely. Monteith saved, and at the same moment Sagar left the field. A centre by Plant brought trouble, but Johnston was at fault. A corner conceded by McDonald was cleared, Notts displaying a robust defence, while Prescott's judgment was exceedingly valuable. Half-time: no score.

Now that Bury had got the wind in their favour it was augured that as before they had more than held their own they would romp in and score a win. They were not, however, allowed any liberty by the Notts' men, and every advantage they secured they had to work for like niggers. The homesters set the pace amid a chorus of plaudits. A corner was unproductive, and Whyte sped along the Notts' right, only, however, to be beaten by Ross. A clever pass by Leeming was negatived by Plant passing too squarely, and Ross cleared. A clever return by Thorpe saw Wood head very weak, and Plant getting possession fired in at a fierce rate, the ball cannoning from a corner. This brought exciting scenes close in goal, the Notts' backs ballooning the ball in disgusting fashion, and once in the melee there were serious appeals for a penalty, but they went unheeded by the referee, Mr. Harrower, who handled the game admirably. Notts paid a visit to Monteith, Green having a chance, but lost it through dallying, while Johnston dashed the ball from his toe. The same half-back started moving again, and Plant made a magnificent shot, which Pennington saved at the cost of a corner. Soon afterwards the ball came out to Richards on the other wing, and, taking aim, he sent the ball spinning into goal. It touched someone in transit, and was flying into the top far corner when ~~Pennington~~ {*Prescott*[19]} fisted it out. A penalty was given in a moment, and **Lindsay**, taking the kick, beat Pennington with a rising shot, which struck underneath the crossbar, and fell over the line. It was never far over, but Mr. Harrower immediately decided this was through, and took no notice of the defenders' desperate efforts to clear. This took place about ten minutes after the interval, and the crowd went simply wild with delight. Now that Bury had once broken the ice they made matters warm for their opponents, and Plant made an incisive wing, while the whole line had sound support from behind. Morris once passed Ross, but Thorpe slipped to the tune of hearty cheering, and the lively Gigg-laners played another merry tune, and Leeming looked likely to score, but Pennington, the old Chorley custodian, saved at close quarters. Since Lindsay's goal Notts had scarcely had a look in. Their forwards seemed utterly unable to negotiate the home halves, and when at last Morris did beat Thorpe, his partner – Whyte – made poor use of his pass. Montgomery cleared strongly after Wood had passed McDonald, and the game now became scrambling, but Notts were entirely out of it, play being almost entirely in their half. Leeming was caught handling close in, but the free kick brought only temporary relief. The play continued in favour of the Bury men right up to the close, but Prescott and Linacre were simply unbeatable, and Bury won.

RESULT: Bury 1 – Notts County 0

BURY: Monteith (goal); Lindsay [1^{pen}] and McEwen (backs); Johnston, Thorpe and Ross (halves); Richards, Lamberton, Sagar, Leeming and Plant (forwards).
NOTTS COUNTY: Pennington (goal); Prescott and Montgomery (backs); Mainman, Bull and McDonald (halves); Whyte, Morris, Green, W. Ross and Gee.
Referee: Mr. Harrower (London).

DERBY COUNTY v. STOKE
at the Baseball Ground, Saturday 7th March, 1903.
Sporting Life - Monday 09 March 1903

No doubt Derby County would much rather have had Notts. Forrest as their opponents in the third round tie at the Baseball Ground at Derby on Saturday, but it is doubtful if they had whether or not they would have fared as well as they did against Stoke, for they gained the most substantial entry into the semi-final stage of any of the four teams. The utmost interest centred in the game in the Midlands, and in the Stoke district in particular there was an amount of sanguinity apparent which led met many to fancy there would be a very different result, for the little Potters were accounted capable of a much better result. The teams had each prepared for the game at home or in the neighbourhood of their headquarters and each was confident. During the week the committee of each side had cripples to trouble them, Bloomer, of the County being bad with an injured knee and under Dr. Warton Hood while Roose was affected, also, with a knee trouble and was in hospital most of the week at Manchester. Bloomer tried his knee on Saturday morning and it broke down, and it was decided that Roose was

---

19 Although this report said Pennington (the goalkeeper), other reports agree that the ball was punched away by full-back Prescott – hence the reason for awarding a penalty.

not fit to play so that both sides laboured under a serious loss, though perhaps that of Stoke was the worst as the amateur is a host in himself and can ill be spared by his side. The weather was none too fine, and the ground difficult to manage. There were about 18,000 people present, some 4000 or 6000 of them having made the journey from Stoke. The Stoke captain won the toss, and Derby had the disadvantages to face.

The opening exchanges were even. Stoke were the first to make the play, Lockett running down his wing and centring, but Morris kicked away finely, and Clark kicked out to stop Warrington. The ground was very heavy and hampered the players movements, but play was keen, and Yorke was given offside close in. Capes got away, but Morris intercepted, and then Methven fouled Lockett, but the free kick was wasted. Stoke were sent back through Locket getting offside, Boag dribbled up, and Davis got in a fine shot, which Burgess headed away. Boag secured again, and put back to **Warren**, who, after seven minutes, scored the opening goal of the match for Derby County amidst an almost deafening round of cheering. Stoke retaliated, but when they were in a fine position Higginson sent over the line. The Potters came again and this time the Derby attack {defence?} had a stiff time of it, Morris and May having all their work cut out to frustrate the Potters. Then Davis fouled Whitehouse as he was about to centre. Morris got the free kick away, and the same player cleared again from a fine centre by the Stoke left wing. The Derby men rushed off to the other end and when Yorke received in a grand position he was adjudged offside, much to the chagrin of the home supporters. But the score was not long in coming. Yorke and Warrington put in some good passing, and when Warrington lifted the ball to the centre of the field **Davis** had little difficulty in rushing in and notching Derby's second goal insight twelve minutes. The Stoke left got in another fine centre, and Morris was lucky to get in the kick which cleared. Yorke got going for the home side, but was adjudged offside. He and Warrington subsequently put in some fine passing, but it was not effective at the finish. Derby were having much the better of matters now, but the game was temporarily delayed through injury to Holford. Derby continued to press, and after Davis had skimmed the bar Yorke forced a corner, and just after that Holford returned. Stoke ran down, and Fryer had to handle from Capes, this being the first time he had been called upon. Derby went back to the other end quickly, but Stoke defended gallantly, and coming back, Whitehouse sent over. Play was fast, considering the heavy ground, but Derby continued to have the best of matters, and after Methven had robbed Capes the County forced a corner. This was followed by another, but the attack ended by Warrington putting behind. Fouls were pretty frequent though not serious. Yorke got the best of a tussle with Clark, but Wilkes kicked away a weak shot without difficulty, and Bradley was robbed through hanging too long on the ball. From a foul by Boag close in Holford shot over, and Morris and May dispossessed the Stoke right when they were working into position. Lockett forced a corner, but Warren and Davis got the ball away. Stoke played up, and Watkins gained another abortive corner. Davis broke away and centred finely, but Boag could not gather the ball, and just missed. The County retaliated but failed to increase their lead. Half-time: Derby County, two goals; Stoke, nil.

The first half had been very much in favour of the home side, and it was now thought they would soon take up a more substantial lead. The Potters were, however, the first to show up with a smart attack, but Methven kicked away, and Boag sent the ball out of danger. Stoke were quickly attacking again, and Whitehouse got in a brilliant centre, only to see Fryer run out and effect a fine clearance before Watkins could get up. Derby retaliated, and forced two corners, and then Wilkes fisted away a fine centre by Yorke and saved a beauty by Boag. Stoke retaliated, but Morris drove them back, and after eleven minutes play **Warrington** received the ball as it bounded off Clark and scored, and thus Derby's third goal was scored. The Stoke men did not lose heart even yet, but played a really fine, plucky game, and kept the home side pegging at it all the way. The Derby defence however, was too good, and they spoilt many movements by too much finesse. However, Higginson at last got in a shot which Fryer saved without much difficulty, and at the other end Burgess headed away a centre by Davis. Derby still pressed and Bury and Yorke went close. Davis and Richards completely bewildered the Stoke defence, but Yorke clean missed a fine chance. Wilkes next saved marvellously from Boag, and by falling on the ball prevented Yorke shooting. Richards brought Wilkes to his knees with a clinking shot, and Warren skimmed the bar. Stoke broke away and Capes sent wide. Fryer saved from Watkins from a foul in the last minute and the game ended in a really clever win for Derby County:

RESULT: Derby County 3 – Stoke 0

DERBY COUNTY: Fryer (goal); Methven and Morris (backs); Warren [1], Goodall and May (halves); Warrington [1], Yorke, Boag, Richards and Davis [1] (forwards).
STOKE: Wilkes (goal); Burgess and Clark (backs); Baddeley, Holford and Bradley (halves); Whitehouse, Higginson, Watkins, Capes and Lockett (forwards).
Referee: Mr. J. Adams (Birmingham).

OTHER RESULTS

07 March 1903
          Millwall 1–0 Everton
       Tottenham Hotspur 2-3 Aston Villa

1902/1903 - The Semi-Finals

Everton's Goodison Park ground at Liverpool was selected as the venue for Bury's semi-final tie, in which they were drawn against Aston Villa, whilst their opponents ground at Villa Park, Birmingham, hosted the other tie between Derby County and Millwall.

As in Bury's past cup-winning season, the semi-finalists were made up of three First League teams and one from the Southern League. All four sides had reached the current stage previously. Millwall, like Bury, just once – that being on the same occasion as Bury in 1900. Only Millwall had never appeared in a Final, whilst Aston Villa had the best record, having reached the final four times with two wins. Millwall's route to the semi-final had been the longest, they having had to enter the competition in the Intermediate round, which match (against Bristol Rovers) had gone to two replays.

Bury's opponents, Villa, had scored the most goals in the previous rounds of the current tournament with 11, whilst Bury had scored the fewest, just 1 in each round (3 in total). The Villa line-up also included a face fondly familiar to Buryites in the form of Jasper McLuckie, who had scored two of the goals that won the trophy for Bury three years earlier. Indeed McLuckie was the leading goalscorer still in the competition, with 5 of Villa's tally of 11. Villa also held the pull in the League encounters that season, garnering three of the four points in contest (winning at Bury and drawing at Villa Park), and were deeply involved in the race for the League championship. Consequently, everywhere outside of Lancashire, Villa were the hot favourites for reaching their fifth final. Bury's best chance seemed to be in their strong half-back line staving off the rampant Villa forwards, in which case snatching another one goal victory might well be hoped for. Bury spent the week training, as usual before important matches, at Lytham, whilst the Villans preferred to prepare at home. On the day of the match, despite the half distance in Bury's case, due to the vagaries of rail travel the two teams journey times to Liverpool would be about the same, the Villans' route being more direct.

In the other tie, Derby County were the clear favourites to reach the final for the third time in six years. Millwall had been lucky in that their three ties in the competition proper, although two of them had been against the toughest opposition in Preston North End and Everton, had all been at home where the peculiarities of their ground had counted greatly in their favour. Derby had also played their three ties to date on their own ground, and had met only one serious contender in Blackburn Rovers, but they had experience on their side, and their best combination of eleven players that had ever contested the competition, although on this occasion they would be without the best of all – Steve Bloomer, who was still out of action after badly injuring his leg in the League match against Blackburn Rovers a month previously.

Both grounds chosen to stage the ties were in tip-top condition and it was confidently expected that the aggregate attendance for both matches would top the 100,000 mark.

BURY v. ASTON VILLA
at Goodison Park, Liverpool – Saturday 21st March, 1903

Athletic News - Monday 23 March 1903
THE VILLA VANQUISHED BY BURY
A Mammoth Assembly at Everton. [By TITYRUS]

The National Cup is famous for the sensational victories and the stupendous surprises it has produced any time during the thirty years, but rarely have League form and recent results been so completely withered up to a mere dry twig of the past as on Saturday at Goodison Park, the home of Everton. There Bury simply annihilated such classic foemen as Aston Villa, who might have been quite a third rate combination instead of one of the most famous teams in the land. Had the Villa been conquered after a heroic struggle by an odd goal there would have been small occasion for astonishment, but they were thrashed entirely, they were outmanoeuvred fore and aft, they were riddled with shots, they were reduced to nonentities, they were smitten hip and thigh, and their supporters were dumbfounded when they sorrowfully wended their way out of the enclosure with Bury victorious by 3-0. The collapse of the Birmingham eleven was so thorough that the older generation were reminded of the rout of Sheffield Wednesday by Blackburn Rovers in a memorable final many years ago. But to be fair to the Wednesday, I must say that the debacle of the villa recalled an occasion when the Wednesday cut up Sunderland at Olive Grove as if they were a school eleven. All honour to Bury for the remarkably effective football they played. The Gigg-lane men have reached the final tie without having a goal scored against them, and whatever be the issue of the last struggle of all, Lancashire is proud of the team, and has reason to be, for they are mostly native, and eight of them are English born. Bury are the despoilers of classic ideals, the iconoclasts of mosaic pattern on beautiful turf, and a most business-like set of workmen, if I may be pardoned by using the language of commerce and trade in connection with the national game. Of course, there are extenuating circumstances to be urged on behalf of the Villa, but first of all let me congratulate Bury on defeating four ex-holders of the Cup off the reel, and that without giving a goal away. Possibly they were Dame Fortune's darlings on Saturday, but the 50,000 people who thronged the enclosure went away with the impression that they had seen a team which never gives their opponents a second's rest, and which believes not in embroidery, not in finesse, not in pretty tactics, but in taking a ticket every time for the goal station. Bury were exhorted by banners to "Buck up" as the last hope of Lancashire, and they obeyed the mandate so well that they swamped their opponents. What could they do more? But the critics are in despair and the small prophets are tearing their hair.

The splendid ground of Everton was in beautiful condition for the best of football, and during the first half we were favoured with a delightful game, in which the play was fast, full of incident, and calculated to please the most exciting enthusiast. The Villa had by far the better of the argument, as they had quite three-fifths of the mid-field manoeuvring in their favour, especially with the breeze to help them. And yet they could not circumvent that gallant defence, and when the breathing time came Bury were one goal up. That is the kind of juggling which the Lancastrians show in Cup-ties. Brawn and Niblo led many a spirited raid, but at the crucial moment either Lindsay or Thorpe interfered, and all the fireworks seemed like a spent skyrocket. We did not see much of

Richards and Wood at this period, but Plant, Leeming, and Sagar were a terrible, bustling and speedy trio, nipping up passes and forging ahead. Once Thorpe sent in a grand lofty ball which George was glad to touch as it flew over the crossbar, for the leather looked like curling underneath. The Villa took many corner-kicks, and most of them beautifully placed, but danger was invariably removed. And in this trying time Montgomery, in goal, proved reliable, even if he occasionally fumbled. But one of these dashes by the Bury left wing brought a goal, for **Plant**, accepting a pass by Sagar, took a long range shot of an oblique character. George was waiting for the ball at one corner of his goal, but, in its swift transit, the leather brushed the legs of Howard Spencer and, turning off at a tangent, rolled quite slowly into the netted space - what time George stood still and powerless, and his comrades were absolutely awe-struck by such an untoward event. It is impossible to deny that this was a lucky goal - and yet the point only showed the wisdom of forwards taking a flying shot, instead of passing and re-passing, and endeavouring to dribble the ball into the haven of rest, the same as the Villa had been trying to do. Of course, they hung on to their chances until one of the Bury players joined in the argument and deprived them. Directly after this goal the Villa attacked, but as Niblo found the net the referee's whistle was sounded for offside. Even after that the Villa were so aggressive that their backs were in Bury territory for a long time. One half of the field was deserted, but Niblo and Pearson had well-meant shots charged down, and Alfred Wood slapped his thigh with vexation as he was half a yard outside the posts. There was some delay ere the game was resumed, for the crowd rushed the barriers and crowded on to the touch lines, Mr. J.C. Clegg, Mr. F.J. Wall, Mr. F.W. Kinder, and Mr. E.A. Lythgoe beseeching the people to stand clear of the chalk lines. Their persuasive appeals were not in vain, and within two minutes of resuming Bury obtained a second goal, for Richards, who began in rare style, middled neatly, and Thorpe pushing the ball forward on the grass, **Sagar** was presented with a nice opportunity, for the defence had been drawn away from him, and he scored in the easiest fashion, while seven minutes later, the issue was placed beyond all doubt by the best goal of the match. Richards and Wood showed some of their most tricky tactics; they walked through the defence, beat both the backs, and **Richards** crowned all the strategic movements by shooting a grand goal with a sharp, low shot. This ended the struggle, for the Villa virtually gave up the ghost, especially as they were for the last half hour without Noon, who was injured on the right knee and had to retire. The Bury forwards threatened danger over and over again, but Spencer and George managed to prevent any more scoring. Thus Bury won by 3-0, the last minutes of the game being little better than a farce, so feebly did the Aston combination perform.

The second period of play was a sorry affair, and hardly seemed part of the game, for the Villa were completely exhausted, and they never looked like partially redeeming themselves with an odd goal.

The winners took as their motto the fashionable word "efficiency," for they completely broke down the Villa defence, and were themselves quite the masters of the Midland attacking brigade. The Bury men were perfectly trained, and they were sound in every department. It was a great handicap for the Lancastrians to be without Hugh Monteith, who, I am told, sustained a slight injury to his ankle whilst at practice on Wednesday. The accident was by no means serious, and although every precaution was taken to ensure his playing, it was felt best to trust a sound man in Montgomery. At times he did not inspire confidence, for he was not too clean in his clearances, but he made a grand dive to keep out one shot in the first half, and he proved a reliable stop-gap. At the same time his backs relieved him of much anxiety, and covered him on every possible occasion. As at Sheffield against the United, Lindsay was a glorious stalwart, and he was strongest when there was the greatest need, his volleying and tackling being quite a feature of the game, even if he did not reach the same standard as at Bramall-lane. McEwen was on his native heath, and gave a display which was remarkable, especially in the second half. But the great strength of Bury was at half back, for Frank Thorpe and Johnston surpassed themselves. There is no doubt that Thorpe completely eclipsed McLuckie, who could do absolutely nothing that was right or serviceable to his side. What is more Thorpe plays football, for he has not to rely on weight, and he does not give one the impression of possessing pace. Yet he has most excellent judgement, and is always in the right place to intercept either with head or foot. His head work is most valuable, and his placing and shooting stamp him as an artist. On their best form there is not much to choose between Booth, Thorpe, and Forman at centre-half. Then Johnson was always intruding with that deft right foot, which seems to pick the ball out and take it away from other people's toes without fail. I have already exhausted my budget of praise for George Ross, who is a worker, and a wonder for his years. The Bury forwards were never exactly brilliant, but they were incisive and hard working. Perhaps Plant and Leeming were the most thrusting, for the former can centre and shoot with here and there one {?}, while Leeming is most industrious and tactical. Rarely does he make a wild pass. Sagar was excellent, and Richards quite at his best in the second half, when he had worn Leake and Noon down, but Wood is not the man we knew. Still, the forwards preserved a capital level of ability without any dazzling star. The whole of the victorious team were genuine triers, fired with real enthusiasm and a never-say-die spirit, while they kept the ball so constantly on the move that they tired the Villa out. Eleven men of good average parts with one set object can accomplish more than many a team with more classic players. The Villa were unfortunate to lose such a worker and such an artist as Joseph Bache, for his absence broke up the line which played so superbly at Tottenham. But he is very ill with the influenza. Then, again, it was questionable policy to play a semi-cripple in Garraty, for he has a weak ankle, and really was so slow that he could hardly raise a gallop. This is not the Garraty we know. Brawn began well, but faded away to a very ordinary performer, while McLuckie was quite useless. The most consistent wing was the left, for Johnson and Niblo tried their best to redeem the situation. But it was not one of Johnson's great days, and Niblo missed Bache, and was apt to over elaboration. The Villa attack was completely mastered, and their half-backs were not able to hold the Bury vanguard. Pearson lacks experience, and to my mind Wilkes could have tried harder and more effectually to keep Plant and his partner in check. Alfred Wood was but middling, while Leake, who was so successful prior to the interval, failed altogether later in the match. For him, Spencer was quite poor, being guilty of hesitancy and kicking to his opponents even near the goal. Noon was far and away the most stubborn defender until he was injured. Indeed, I have never seen Noon take the ball so cleanly, and it must be remembered that the Bury forwards never gave a back a free kick if they could possibly get on to him. Then I understand that George has been suffering from three abscesses under his left arm, and these were cut on Friday. A man in such a condition was not fit to keep goal, and, I think, proved it, for George rarely showed that saving grace which usually distinguishes him.

RESULT: Bury 3 – Aston Villa 0

BURY: Montgomery (goal); Lindsay and McEwen (backs); Johnston, Thorpe and Ross (halves); Richards [1], Wood, Sagar [1], Leeming and Plant [1] (forwards).
ASTON VILLA: George (goal); Spencer and Noon (backs); Pearson, Wood and Leake (halves); Brawn, Garraty, McLuckie, Johnson and Niblo (forwards).
Referee: Mr. P. R. Harrower (London).

DERBY COUNTY v. MILLWALL
at Villa Park, Birmingham – Saturday 21st March, 1903
Athletic News - Monday 23 March 1903
MILLWALL LION'S LAST ROAR.
The Tale of a Fatal Sky-Rocket. [By NONDESCRIPT]

{Warning – as a historical record the following report is reproduced verbatim but contains a word and an allusion that may now be considered racially offensive.}

Our match at Birmingham was a disappointment in the sense that it discovered such a marked discrepancy between the merits of the rival parties. If asked whether this was due to an unfortunate accident which befell Millwall just when a nice prospect was being opened for them, or whether they were beaten by an altogether better side, I should certainly advance this latter reason. Fact of the matter is that friend Leo from Thames-side had his tail badly trodden upon, was finally chained up securely, and though he roared louder than any sucking dove, or eke nightingale, never got a single bite at his tormentors. Millwall for the second time in a creditable career are, to use a familiar term, "not class enough" to adorn this stage of the competition, and while this was made most manifest at Saturday's function the fact was established too early in the afternoon to please the patrons of Aston Villa's spacious enclosure. Else the affair was a success. Save that the wind blew with infinite gusto, it was a beautiful spring day, and the crowd was a gigantic one. The majority of the big wigs of the Association world apparently had hied themselves northward, yet there were many notabilities past and present on the ground, and the portion which goes by the name of the paddock was redolent with the perfumes of Sweet Williams - the chieftain McGregor - who, and Mr. Ramsey were masters of the ceremonies and who, after a heavy afternoon's labours, had to bear the weight of doleful tidings from Liverpool; W. I. Bassett, looking not a day older than when he last skipped the lines at Stoney-lane; last, but not least, bluff Will Holbrook, who had taken French leave of his favourite Foresters for one brief afternoon, and who was in charge of a party of Nottingham celebrities, and sprinkling all and sundry with dashes of home-brewed sauce. There were others, too, who were wanderers from the home fireside, for a deputation of Liverpool officials had left the big game at Goodison just to come down and make arrangements for the League match with Derby County on Monday, you know. Another link with football of the past turned up in Alfred Albut, who formerly handled the reins at Newton Heath. An old timer who "could a tale unfold" has a notion some day of writing a book - 'Wheels within Wheels of Football Management,' or some such title - and thinks with the collaboration of one Parlby, of Manchester, he could make it an entertaining theme. By all means let us have it. Altogether it was a great assembly, but the entertainment which followed was quite unworthy of the occasion.

The winning of the toss was a distinct advantage to Millwall, for the breeze, if it seemed to run into corkscrew variations at times, was in the main blowing from goal to goal. The Southerners were early astir, too, in an endeavour to turn this to account, and until they were overcome by the cruel stroke of misfortune, which will be the topic of conversation in dockyard circles for many a day, we saw the real Cup-fighting team on parade, showing off points calculated to disturb the equanimity of even the best conducted League eleven. Pioneer in chief in a number of dashing raids, Moran gave promise of being a very important factor in the afternoon's ceremonies, yet somehow from this good beginning the little man fell away to such an extent that he had become an almost insignificant atom long before the close. With a dry ground and a lively ball we plunged into incident right away. The Millwall box of tricks just mentioned won a corner single-handedly, and put the ball so beautifully across that Bell headed on to the bar. The other goal underwent an even narrower escape than this, for, from a second corner to Millwall, Davis made ground so admirably on the Derby left that he was able at last to put the ball across midway between Sutcliffe and Storrier, and with such judgement and pace that both were helpless. The back was at fault, for he left his wing entirely unmarked. He got off with a caution, for Warrington was in too desperate a hurry altogether, and fired over. Hot business at the Derby end, where Morris, with a little good luck on his side, intercepted a "traveller," and Moran was just too late to trap another, and then came the sensation of the day. Storrier, hard pressed, kicked into touch. **Warren**, taking the throw-in, had the ball tapped back by a colleague, and with the kick of a mule sent it careering into the heavens. That a goal would result without the intervention of another player could not for a moment have been imagined by anyone. It was 60 a yards' drive both in length and altitude. Had there been no wind to develop check action the ball must have flown over the cycle track, and reached the crowd. A bow at a venture working such devastation in the ranks of the enemy was surely never drawn in this particular class of warfare. With the exception of Sutcliffe there was not a man in the vicinity of the goal, but something told the keeper that there was danger lurking in that ball as it stopped suspended in mid air, and he made a dash to field it. Striking the full glare of the sun, however, he misjudged the matter altogether. The attempt for a magnificent catch was just what one imagines old Rugby expert such as he would delight in. But he got too far out - so far as to ruin all chances of recovering himself - and there was a spectacle of a great custodian away from his post, helpless, watching a ball which bounced right in front of goal, and then lobbed through. Fancy the luck of the thing! If Sutcliffe had never moved he would just have had an ordinary handful. Amazement at this catastrophe was written on the face of every man in the Dockers' team. Ere they had time to fairly pull round another shaft was driven home amongst them. The dramatic incident just alluded to occurred after eight minutes. In less than another five minutes Derby had well secured their entry to the final. Goodall, playing one of the games of his life, paved the way, and then Warren, who was all along combining the slimness of a Boer with the ferocity a tiger, emerged with honours from a battle royal with Gettins, and set Warrington on the run. The wing man put across to Yorke, whose shot, a straight one well seasoned with mustard, cannoned off Storrier, **Boag** fastening on the rebound and scoring with another hot ball which Sutcliffe just touched but had no chance of stopping. There was no luck attaching to the success. It was industriously, cleverly, striven for, and worthily earned. Another move, equally well thought out, in all save the penultimate stroke which put Warrington offside, showed the incisive character of the Derby attack. Even with four forwards they held their own for the last twenty minutes of the opening half. During that period they were without Davis, who, caught on one leg as he was endeavouring to keep the ball in play, was bundled neck and crop over the line by Moran, and fell so awkwardly on the cycle track that he lost consciousness for some time. This band of cement at the Aston grounds is altogether too near the field of play. The charge appeared to be legitimate enough, though Moran, on the appeal of the linesman, was penalised. Try as they would, Millwall could not wrest back any of the lost ground, even though the opposition were outmanned and were operating against the wind. They gave Fryer a fair amount of work - as a matter of fact he had as much employment found him during the afternoon than Sutcliffe - but at the same time he was not over taxed. Once from a free kick Easton placed the ball so accurately that it struck the underside of the crossbar and fell into the arms of the keeper, who threw away. Moran also made a capital attempt, while absolutely the best shot of the afternoon came from Astley. The ball was going away from Fryer all the time, but it was just on the wrong side of the post. From one of several corners which they took Millwall had their last chance with the wind, and only a clever back-handed save of Fryer's frustrated them.

At change of ends the position for them was hopeless. Derby boarded full strength again; indeed Davis, after his short sojourn in dreamland, seemed to be filled with all sorts of clever ideas, and in the second half was as smart a man as any on the field. The best shot of the afternoon by Millwall was supplemented with the most brilliant single-handed run. This was where Watkins shone. It was a giant's effort, and it deserved a better fate, but Jones, whom he placed in possession, described the wrong angle with the goal. To this **Richards** replied with a clever hook shot which secured Derby's third point, and people began to leave the ground while there was yet half an hour to go. Millwall got plenty of the ball, it is true, but every time the Derby front laid themselves down to real work their superiority was manifest, and with interest in the proceedings having gone spark out no one was sorry when the end came.

I imagine that the Millwall people from the outlet recognised that they had more on hand than they could satisfactorily accomplish. But they were not so poor in heart after beating Everton - however did they manage to do it? - as to be without hope of "something turning up." The spin of the coin was a strong point in their favour, and the manner in which they set about their business in the first seven or eight minutes encouraged the idea that the County had found worthy foemen. The Southerners got most of the ball during this period, distributed it with some intelligence, and evidently meant to rush their opponents with all the superiority in physique which the former could command. The next hour, however, found them out, and in the end they were proven to be considerably wanting in those qualities which go to make up a first-class team. That the circumstance of Sutcliffe's misfielding that ball of Warren's reduced them to static temporary paralysis was evident enough. It was a veritable bolt from the blue. To my mind the custodian was partly to blame, and partly to be sympathised with. If he stayed in goal he was giving the enemy a fine open field for attack in front. His backs were not at hand; furthermore, I suspect that he had lost some confidence in Storrier after the latter's faulty judgment shown in the first three minutes. He had to deal with a shot the like of which troubles a keeper only once or twice in a lifetime. The original mistake arose in failing to gauge the flight of the ball, and it was a double blunder because if it was his idea that the wind would carry it back towards the centre he should have left the matter for someone else to attend to. The glint of the sun completed his discomfiture. It is something new to see Sutcliffe beaten thrice and never up to that point having been called upon for a thrilling save. Later he showed some of the resource of old, but I fear that his display altogether will jeopardise his chances of appearing against the Scots, and this may be his misfortune rather than his fault, for I believe he is not thoroughly recovered from a kick on the head received in a recent match. The Millwall backs were inconsistent, sometimes stemming a threatening advance by sheer application of *avoirdupois*[20], with which both Easton and Storrier are well endowed and sometimes performing slovenly. Watkins was the outstanding figure in a half-back line which was considerably below the level of the Derby trio, and this player is more than useful. The other two began well, and Bell in the first half-hour was responsible for some nice passes to his forwards, but the longer the game ran and the greater did Goodall and May prevail against them. The forwards were energetic enough and very frequently clever, failing, however, to turn their good work to advantage. It is a pity more was not seen of Moran, for he is a delightful chap to follow, but he unmistakably fought shy of Morris. The last-named knew that if he offered the slightest opening the ball would go plump into goal every time, so the Welshman with judicious application of weight came to be the master of the situation. Hulse, in his zeal, was inclined to roam at times, but his whole-heartedness goes hand-in-hand with considerable ability, and is a tough customer to engage with when in possession. Gettins, as usual, worked like a nigger. But it was late in the afternoon ere he loomed up against Fryer, and then out of an awkward situation his shot, though going straight for an unprotected part, had no powder behind it, and was easily attended to. Astley and Jones were just fair members of a line and of a whole team generally, which must be more than useful in its own class. That, however, does not approach the standard of the League. Millwall, in short, are no better than when I last saw them in a semi-final. "Third time pays for all," they say, and so Derby should win the Cup. But after the crushing blow administered to Aston Villa, who would have been a match at Tottenham the other week for an international team, I respectfully decline to soar into the realms of prophecy. Perseverance perhaps will have its reward. For my own part I should very much like to see the Midlanders gain their ambition. With stolid defence and halves and forwards who understand each other they are a good, workmanlike lot, when seen, as was the case here, in one of their best humours, but they subscribe to some of the atrocities of football when they do get off colour. It is curious that the team carries more ballast when Bloomer is absent. The forwards certainly get over the ground with a more harmonious swing, and including as they did on Saturday one substitute and a veteran, their's was a much better idea than was shown by Millwall of what a movement was likely to result in. In their time Derby have tried many centre forwards, but Boag seems to be the one and only relieving officer when Cup-ties require serious discussions. He is not a star, just a good honest plodder, very often popping up at the right moment, and doing the right thing, and he had some good men on either side of him, notably Richards, who was only inspired to renewed endeavour such time as he lost his partner, and Davis, who pleased me immensely. The latter would not disgrace a representative company. The Derby halves played a great, a tremendous worrying game, with Archie Goodall the masterpiece. He and Methven are marvels of ability and

---

20 Avoirdupois – to apply weight/force (from old English system of weight measurement).

endurance, and an English Cup medal apiece after all these years of valiant service will be a fitting reward in the evening of their football lives.

RESULT: Derby County 3 – Millwall 0

DERBY CO.: Fryer (goal); Methven and Morris (backs); Warren, Goodall and May (halves); Warrington, Yorke, Boag, Richards and Davis (forwards).
MILLWALL: Sutcliffe (goal); Easton and Storrier (backs); Riley, Bell and Watkins (halves); Moran, Astley, Hulse, Gettins and R. Jones (forwards).
Referee: Mr. J. Lewis (Blackburn).

THE CARBOLIC SMOKE BALL
WILL POSITIVELY CURE
HAY FEVER.

HAY FEVER is a disease from which many people suffer during the most pleasant season of the year, and one which renders their lives miserable.
HAY FEVER makes its presence known by incessant fits of sneezing, followed by a flow of hot transparent mucus from the nostrils, accompanied by a burning sensation and watering eyes. The soothing action of the CARBOLIC SMOKE BALL upon the membrane allays all irritation, gradually arrests the hot flow from the nostrils and eyes, and stops the sneezing and burning sensation.
The CARBOLIC SMOKE BALL will positively cure, and is the only remedy ever discovered which has permanently cured HAY FEVER, a disease that has hitherto baffled the skill of the most eminent physicians, who have sought in vain to cure or prevent its annual return.

THE CARBOLIC SMOKE BALL
WILL ALSO CURE

INFLUENZA · CATARRH · THROAT DEAFNESS · CROUP
COUGHS · ASTHMA · SORE THROAT · WHOOPING COUGH
COLDS · BRONCHITIS · LOSS OF VOICE · NEURALGIA
COLD ON THE CHEST · HOARSENESS · SNORING · HEADACHE

As all the diseases mentioned above either arise from, or are aggravated by one cause, viz., TAKING COLD, they can, therefore, be cured by the remedy which stops the cause, viz.: The CARBOLIC SMOKE BALL.
One CARBOLIC SMOKE BALL will last a family several months, making it the cheapest remedy in the world at the price—10s., post free.
The CARBOLIC SMOKE BALL can be refilled, when empty, at a cost of 5s., post free.

CARBOLIC SMOKE BALL CO., LTD.
27, PRINCES STREET, HANOVER SQUARE, LONDON, W.

1902/1903 - The Final

BURY

DERBY

Player Comparisons

Name	Nat.	Age	Height	Weight	Position	Weight	Height	Age	Nat.	Name
Monteith	SC	25	5'10½"	13/0	Goal	13/8	6'2½"	26	EN	Fryer
Lindsay	EN	23	5'9½"	13/2	Right Back	12/8	5'9"	34	SC	Methven
McEwen	EN	29	5'6"	11/0	Left Back	12/0	5'8"	23	EN	Warren
Johnston	EN	25	5'8½"	10/12	Right Half	13/0	5'10½"	22	WA	Morris
Thorpe	EN	22	6'0"	11/9	Centre Half	12/4	5'7"	38	IR	Goodall
Ross	SC	33	5'9"	12/8	Left Half	10/10	5'7½"	25	SC	May
W. Richards	EN	24	5'7"	11/4	Outside Right	10/6	5'7½"	21	EN	Warrington
Wood	EN	24	5'7½"	11/8	Inside Right	12/8	5'11"	21	SC	Yorke
Sagar	EN	22	5'11½"	11/8	Centre Forward	12/1	5'9"	29	SC	Boag
Leeming	EN	27	5'9½"	11/12	Inside Left	10/10	5'8½"	22	EN	G. Richards
Plant	EN	32	5'8½"	12/2	Outside Left	10/12	5'6½"	21	EN	Davis
		26	5'9"	11/13	Average	11/13	5'8"	25		

THE GOALKEEPERS

BURY: HUGH MONTEITH was born at New Cumnock, Ayrshire, and is 25 years of age. His early football was learned with the Parkhead juniors, after which he joined the Celtic. Loughborough next engaged him, while after assisting Bristol City he became custodian for West Ham United. Monteith is nimble and active, and, having a varied experience, is quite at home in first class company, Bury are quite pleased with him.

DERBY CO.: JOHN SPENCER FRYER, is one of the tallest custodians in the league and on his day one of the best. Makes the most of his height and reach, and his display in a Cup tie at Wolverhampton five years ago is spoken of as one of the best ever seen. Friar was born at Cromford 26 years ago, and has been with Derby County since 1897.

THE RIGHT BACKS

BURY: JAMES LINDSAY was born at Stockton in 1879. Played local football before signing for Newcastle united in 1899 but failed to gain any prominence on Tyneside before transferring to Burnley where he first began to make his name. Came to Bury towards the end of the 1900/01 season, and made an immediate impact on the side. Known as a rare good tackler who sticks well to his work, and is the speediest man in the side, having won several medals as a professional sprinter.

DERBY CO.: JAMES METHVEN is a player of great experience and skill. Is a remarkably clever tackler and his coolness is imperturbable. He was born at Perth, and had played first class football with Edinburgh St. Bernard's when 17 years of age. Also turned out a few times for Leith Athletic and Heart of Midlothian. After turning down an approach from Burton Swifts he subsequently came south of the border to join the County. That was some eleven years ago, making him now the elder statesman of the side. Not as fast as he once was but plays with a cool confidence and calm assurance that makes him a hard man to beat.

THE LEFT BACKS

BURY: JAMES 'Punch' McEWEN was born at Liverpool of Irish parentage. He first played for Lansdowne, Bootle, and Liverpool South End, subsequent to which he was tried by Everton. He then migrated to Luton, where he made a big name for himself. Glossop subsequently had the benefit of his services, and finally he signed on for Bury at the beginning of last season. He's one of the most popular members of the team, and, though lacking in inches and height, is a fearless tackler and kicks well with either foot, whilst his quick dashes are quite a feature of his play.

DERBY CO.: BENJAMIN WARREN, is a representative of local talent, having been born at Newhall, Derbyshire. He is a perfect glutton for work, and in Cup matches is seen at his best, playing for all he is worth the whole ninety minutes. Last season he gained some notoriety as a forward by his go getting proclivities in Cup-ties, but he is doing well this year by fearless work at halfback. This is his fourth season with the County.

THE RIGHT HALVES

BURY: JOHN SHAND JOHNSTON counts himself a Lancashire lad although he was actually born at Cumpsie, in Scotland, before coming to the County Palatine as an infant when his father relocated the family to the Wigan district where he had found work. Learned his football with the Handley club and Stalybridge Rovers before joining Bury two seasons ago as an 'A' team player. As an emergency man he was first tried in the first eleven at right half-back, and, showing considerable ability, was at length included in the team permanently. He is a right-sided defender of the terrier type, and, without being brilliant, gets through a tremendous amount of work.

DERBY CO.: CHARLES 'Charlie' MORRIS is, of course, the Welsh International full-back, and is believed by many good judges to be unsurpassed in that position. Tackles with unerring precision, and takes the ball in all positions. He was born at Oswestry, and came to Derby from the Church club in 1900. Played in all three internationals this season with signal success.

THE CENTRE HALVES

BURY: FRANK THORPE is another adoptive Lancastrian having been born just across the Derbyshire border at Glossop. He came to Bury from Stalybridge Rovers, and, though previously tried at Newton Heath, was not thought much of. Tall and rangy, he has improved wonderfully since his arrival at Gigg-lane and is now the personification of coolness, whilst no half-back feeds his forwards with better judgment. Is held in great estimation by his fellow players both on and off the field. Has few superiors at centre-half whilst he has also achieved moderate success as a stand-in centre-forward.

DERBY CO.: ARCHIBALD 'Archie' GOODALL (captain), has been playing the best class of football for a matter of fifteen years, and is quite the veteran of the First Division of the League. For all he is still a great player, a superb tackler, and a fine judge of pace. He has captained the County since brother John went to Glossop. Also captain's the Irish team, having been born at Belfast, when his father, a soldier, was stationed there. Played this year against England and Wales, and scored a goal against the latter from half-back. Is a lifelong teetotaller and non-smoker.

THE LEFT HALVES

BURY: GEORGE 'Geordie' ROSS, the senior member of the team, is a Scotsman by birth, but has spent all but twelve months of his life in Lancashire. Ross *pere* was a constable, and left his native place to join the Lancashire County Constabulary. From Preston the family migrated to Bury, where some sixteen or seventeen years ago George began playing football with the Bury Wesleyan club. He was not long in seclusion, joining the Bury club some twelve years ago, before even the organisation became connected with the Lancashire League. He has for all this dozen years been a steady and consistent player. "Men may come, and men may go, but George goes on for ever," they have begun to say in Bury. He has played in practically every match since his club got into the First Division of the League. He's getting on, for he has reached thirty, but there is yet a lot of good football in him.

DERBY CO.: JOHN MAY, is a Scotsman, with international ambitions. He was born at Paisley, and played North of the border with the Paisley Abercorn Club before joining Derby County in 1896. Since then has developed into one of the finest half-backs in the game. A fine tackler and a difficult man to pass who played the game scientifically, often reversing the play by a clever pass to his forwards. Has been unlucky in getting injured frequently, but is playing very well just now.

THE OUTSIDE RIGHTS

BURY: WILLIAM 'Billy' RICHARDS is another Lancashire lad. He was born at Heaton Park, and at the age at 18 played for Middleton Parish Church. He subsequently joined Tonge, a Lancashire Alliance eleven, and then migrated to play for Middleton in the Lancashire League. He was tried by Bury at the end of season 1899/1900 and was introduced to the Bury side in time to play a substantial role in the following season's F.A. Cup campaign.

DERBY CO.: JOSEPH 'Joe' WARRINGTON is a fair haired youth who first saw the light at Macclesfield, and who was drafted into the County ranks from the Derby Cedars Club. Is lightly built, but has shaped well and scored his fair share of goals in his two seasons with the County. Capable of playing anywhere in the front line but prefers, and serves his club best, at outside-right.

THE INSIDE RIGHTS

BURY: WILLIAM WOOD is another Middleton lad and a good friend of Billy Richards with whom he played on the right wing for the Middleton town club before the pair joined Bury at the end of last season. Hence, although both are in their first season at Gigg-lane, their own right wing pairing is well established – although they have traded positions since their Middleton days, Wood going inside and Richards out. Missed much of the early part of the current season due to injury.

DERBY CO.: CHARLES H. YORKE, is a native of Edinburgh, and came to Derby last summer from Reading. Can play in all the forward positions with some success and is the go to man when any of the regular forwards are unavailable. Included in the Cup Final side as a substitute for Bloomer. His particular forte is the first time shot on the run by which he frequently surprises opposing custodians.

THE CENTRE FORWARDS

BURY: CHARLES SAGAR, the inside man of the team is another member of the old Turton Club. He began his football career with the Turton St. Anne's Sunday School Club, then members of the Bolton and District Sunday School. He later on played for Turton and in April, 1898, took up his post in the Bury organisation. Since then he has rapidly come to the front. He was selected as reserve man for England against Scotland last season. As a matter of fact he has played one international game this season against Ireland, and scored one of the goals.

DERBY CO.: JOHN BOAG is a native of Glasgow, and before joining the County club played for East Stirlingshire. Joined County during the 1896/97 season but initially was not a success. Eventually showed his worth a year later when he scored a hat trick in a Cup tie against Liverpool after being recalled to the side due to an injury crisis. Is now a mainstay of the side. Neither flamboyant nor especially skilled but plays with a directness and energy that regularly breaks through opposition defences.

THE INSIDE LEFTS

BURY: JOE LEEMING was born at Preston and raised at Turton where he served his footballing apprenticeship with the village team before joining Bury five seasons past. In his time with the club has proved to be a capital all round player, capable of playing in any division of the field except goal – but prefers to play up front on the left. Receives and passes the ball well and shoots hard at goal.

DERBY CO.: GEORGE H. RICHARDS hails from Castle Donington, and is a product of the County club's search for local talent. He came to County's attention last season whilst playing for the Whitwick White Cross Club against the Derby County reserve XI in the Midland Counties League. Was immediately snapped up as a reserve team player and has since justified all expectations. After a single outing with the first eleven towards the end of last season he got his big chance last October when the side was shaken up following the injury to May, and has kept his place in the side ever since.

THE OUTSIDE LEFTS

BURY: JOHN PLANT junior, the outside left, is a Cheshire Lad, having been born at Bollington, near macclesfield, and played with the Bollington Club prior to joining Bury some twelve years ago. Until the season 1897-8 Plant was a regular member of the Bury team, but he then took a fit for a change, and played for Reading in the season 1898-9, but he came home again this season and has done good work for the team. He has participated in all Bury's big games, including the 1900 Cup Final, and is proud of his team.

DERBY CO.: GEORGE H. DAVIS, a new man but a good one and another product of the search for local talent, being a native of Alfreton, Derbyshire. Has been showing fine form as a partner for Richards on the left wing. He is a capital dribbler, moving quickly and drawing opponents before releasing the ball to his centre-forward. Can also play at half-back but has had bad luck through injuries when playing in that position.

Notably absent from the Derby side was **Steve Bloomer**, *who failed a late fitness test from the injury he had suffered against Blackburn in February and which had kept him out of the side since. It was a significant loss since Steve was one of the most prolific goalscorers of his era.*

Bloomer was a native of the Black Country, being born at Cradley, near Halesowen, although his family moved to the Derby area when he was still a small child. After playing minor football in the Derby area he was a 17 year old playing for Derby Midland when that club merged with Derby County in 1891. After a year in the reserves he got his chance in the County first team at the start of the 1892/93 season and grabbed it with both hands, finishing the season as County's second highest goalscorer. After that he was consistently the club's top scorer for the next nine seasons leading up to the 1903 Cup Final (and on the way to his 10th such achievement), and had played in both of County's previous unsuccessful finals. He was also an England International who in the course of his career would go on to accumulate twenty-three England caps (an enormous number for the period) scoring 28 goals in the process.

Before the Match

As always, the Cup Final aroused a great deal of interest throughout the country. For many, especially in the Midlands, Derby County were accounted the popular favourites, not least because it was felt that their time was well past due. Over the previous eight years they had reached the final on two prior occasions and the semi-final stage four times more without ever carrying off the spoils. Bury, on the other hand, could be said to have a 100% record in a similar respect, having carried off the trophy on the only occasion they had reached so far as the latter two stages. On this occasion Bury had certainly had the tougher route to the final, their opponents at every stage being not only First Division sides but also former winners of the trophy. Derby counted a Second Division side and a Southern League side amongst their opponents, and only one former winner of the trophy. The latter, however, had been the Blackburn Rovers, at that time the greatest cup fighters of all, with their name inscribed on the trophy no fewer than five times.

Bury had no significant injury doubts ahead of the game and spent the week prior in gentle training whilst enjoying the sea air at Lytham. Team selection was confirmed on Wednesday (April 15th) and the players, in the charge of Messrs. Wardle, Duckworth and Unsworth, departed for the capital on Thursday by the 8:30 a.m. train. The party arrived in London just after 3:00 p.m. and were transported by a four horse brake[21] to the White Swan Hotel, facing the Palace at Upper Norwood, where they were to stay until the time for the match. Following the match they were to stay at the Tavistock Hotel, Covent Garden until Monday morning before leaving for the Midlands for a postponed League match at West Bromwich Albion.

Derby made their final preparations at home, although following their away match at Middlesbrough the previous weekend they had spent a couple of days in training further up the North-East coast at Tynemouth. Hopes of Bloomer returning to the side were dashed after his ankle failed a test on Thursday whilst there were injury concerns also over Fryer and Methven, whilst Archie Goodall was in mourning after receiving the news on Wednesday of his mother's death at Kilmarnock. Consequently Davies, reserve goalkeeper; Lloyd, reserve half-back; and Middleton, reserve forward, all travelled with the team, accompanied by the directors and manager Mr. Newbould, that left Derby by the 3p.m. Midland Express for St. Pancras on Friday afternoon, their London headquarters being the Inns of Court Hotel at Holborn.

With no Southern side in the final there was little prospect of a record crowd at a Crystal Palace ground which had undergone several improvements ahead of the event. The number of crush barriers on the raised banks surrounding the playing area had been greatly increased, a new stand had been erected behind the North goal, significantly increasing the capacity of covered seating, and no fewer than 70 new turnstiles had been installed around the ground making ingress to the stadium easier than ever before to eliminate any crush on the approaches. The pitch, meanwhile, was in tip-top condition – green, level and springy – just right for a fast game.

---

21 Passenger carriage with bench seats arranged lengthways on either side.

BURY v. DERBY COUNTY
At Crystal Palace, London – Saturday 18th April, 1903
Sporting Life - Monday 20th April, 1903
THE COUNTY BADLY DEFEATED.
JUST ESTABLISH TWO RECORDS.
(BY OUR OWN REPORTER.)

Never in the history of the Football Association Cup has any club suffered such a sweeping defeat as did Derby County on Saturday last at the classic Crystal Palace ground. The victory gained by Bury with six goals to nothing came as one of those surprises which in sport sometimes will occur, but in this one particular case it was a matter of the stronger combination triumphing over the weaker, and the Lancastrians are fully entitled to all the honours of the day and congratulations which were showered upon their capless heads. By defeating the County as they did Bury create a record for themselves, and by going through the competition without having a single point registered against them, a record of which they will be justly proud for many a long day to come. For the vanquished there can only be a feeling of sorrow for the most part, for the reason that luck has often been against them in Cup games, but on Saturday it was generally known that at least two members of the team were what is known in high society as "off colour." No side can possibly go to the field with perfect confidence and a knowledge that their chief means of defence is on the crocked list, but with the dogged determination to do or die J.S. Fryer undertook to do his level best. Unfortunately, as the sequel showed, he was prevented by accident from even accomplishing that, and all sportsmen will be with us in wishing him a speedy recovery from the affects of his terrific collision with Sagar early in the second half. To that fact alone can the long list of goal scoring be attributed, for, although Morris was substituted, yet he was nothing like so clever as the other man.

THE INVASION OF LONDON

Whether they had counted them individually or by the trainload is somewhat uncertain, but anyhow one enterprising journal assured its readers that over 30,000 visitors had reached London by eleven o'clock in the morning, and this was very probably true, for all the big stations at Euston, the Great Central, King's Cross, and St. Pancras were besieged with train loads of tired but contented humanity from break of day, and the Euston-road and adjacent neighbourhood was absolutely alive with North countrymen of all classes, shapes, and sizes. Up above the tramp of the wooden shoon[22] is music, but when applied to the pavements of London there was something else required to create that harmony pleasing to a musician's ear. It was not forthcoming, but something else was, which if not music, was calculated to change the colour of the atmosphere to that of the Lancastrians' shirts. "Oh, it's awful!" remarked one pious lady to another on the top of the bus; and, well, there! the least said about it the better. Perhaps some day poor Londoners will be educated up to the high level of proficiency in languages evidently reigning in northern climes. Of course the visitors wanted nourishment, and, by Jingo, some of them had it, with a vengeance. How many will get on the black list has not yet been recorded, but one would hope the good feeling existing between

---

22 Shoon – [archaic] Plural of shoe.

workers in Lancashire and Derbyshire would prevent such dire calamity as allowing fellow creature to remain in town at Government expense. There is no mistake about it; rough may be the outside appearance of the average miner, but within beats a heart as big as a football, and, what is more, when sport is concerned, he can hold his own with the best of us. Unlike the southerner, he abhors tilling the soil, but is perfectly agreeable to delve into the bowels of the earth two or three days in the week, while enjoying the result of his time, watching or indulging in sport. Every man has his hobby, and while the majority are owners and experts on whippets, such diverting amusements as clog dancing, concertina playing, coddam[23], and the use of the gloves, to say nothing of rat killing, badger baiting, and others provided amusement for the many who attended the Palace on Saturday. Then again it is the fact that although every one of them is not a "Datas[24]," get an enquiry as to when any certain horse won the Derby, or who was the winner of the Waterloo Cup in any particular year, will be answered as readily as though our own "AUGER" or "LAMBOURNE"[25] were invited to reply. It's born in 'em and will ever remain. The difference between the sporting instinct of North and South is indeed very great amongst the working class, and only the other day the writer heard of a gentleman who made a bet with another that he would enquire from the first countryman he met within three miles of Goodwood if he knew the course, and receive a response in the negative. He did, and the reply was, "I can't tell-ee zur. I 'arnt bin livin' yer but three yeer." No; rough and ready, reliant and sportive to a degree, is the order of the North, and no wonder even in football if we have to draw on their resources. Those who don't follow the game must have been surprised to see so many bedecked with either red and black or light blue - the latter we take it as compliment to Cambridge for having won sports and boat race - or with a bunch of primroses in their coats, emblematical of the great respect in which the memory of the great Beaconsfield[26] is held, promenading the streets, while their wonderment would be still more when they noted the hundreds of fully laden brakes assembled at various starting points. Thousands hadn't been before, and naturally they wanted to see the sights, so the majority made excursions before reaching the Palace.

THE BUILD UP

Once inside the majority looked and felt strange, for the huge Crystal House is hardly a place one can feel at home in on the first visit. However, the grand organ peeled forth, and to the Northerner nothing can appeal with more force, so many of them stayed and listened, while others walked around, and, under the seductive attractions of the various stallholders, filled their pockets with little nicknacks to take home t'kids. Once down the staircase and long rows of steps the huge crowd quickly lined up around the spacious enclosure, and, as usual, the scene became one that must ever live in the memory of any who have attended the Final tie. Picture the amphitheatre, with a living study in black and white; while free from the crowded Pavilion a fine view of spectators, tier above tier, until, still further back, the long line of trees radiant in their new green costumes, and studded with human faces, and the great open space on which the

---

23 Coddam – a popular gambling game played in public houses.
24 Datas – repository of information.
25 AUGER and LAMBOURNE – pseudonyms of two sports writers.
26 Beaconsfield – Benjamin Disraeli, former P.M., 1st Earl of Beaconfsfield (whose badge was the primrose).

game is played, and you have some idea of the Palace ground. True, there was an occasional touch of colour, and even the white tents decreased the somber hue of the crowd; but gentle spring is not so far advanced as to allow with safety the departure from winter to summer clothing, and with a somewhat low temperature, the majority were well advise to turn out prepared for the worst, doubtless remembering the snowstorm of a few years back. To those who haven't seen it, the Crystal Palace crowd is a perfect source of wonder, and probably the best tempered in the world. Police are there in force of course to keep order if wanted, but during the last seven years it has been the writers good fortune to attend the same function, it has never been his lot to witness a single arrest, even although being here, there, and everywhere. No, as a rule visitors come to see the match, and that over they are generally content to depart in peace and enjoy the remaining hours till train time arrives. The nimble pickpocket is apparently a stranger, and the only trouble arises when the bottle has been applied too often, but even here, with over 63,000 persons, the majority of whom have been stived[27] up in a railway carriage for several hours, there are but few cases of intoxication, and those who do fall under the influence generally manage to sleep through until the finish, so that even that fearful searchlight, which has for years been a terror to young couples who "breathe sweet nothings in each other's ear" after dark, is not now required to locate them.

Armed with the very necessary "brief," without which none are admitted, a tour of inspection to the Pavilion is always necessary, and so in company with a fellow scribe, the severe janitors at the door were safely passed. And then one felt there was something wanting; it didn't seem quite the same; and we then remembered the cheery smile of a face, now alas no more, that of one of the most obliging and courteous of managers, Mr. Henry Gillman, whose hearty shake of the hand year by year made one feel quite at home so soon as the open portal had been passed. Unfortunately his familiar figure was not the only one missing, for on looking round another had left a vacant space. One, who although a leading light in the Rugby game, never failed to put in an appearance at the Association Cup Final. Reference is of course made to the recent lamented death of Mr. R.S. Whalley, whose memory will ever linger in the hearts of a large number of friends. With two North Country clubs engaged there were of course a host of others one would hardly expect to see, but amongst those who are prominent the writer recognised Lord Kinnaird, Mr. G.S. Sherrington, Mr. C.T. Clegg, Mr. S.R. Spofforth, Mr. Malcom Roberts, Sir Thomas Roe, Steve Bloomer (who was unfortunately unable to assist his side), Mr. H.W. Lawson, Mr. H.W. Wilson, Mr. Phil Gilliard, Mr. F.J. Wall (the height of courtesy under very difficult conditions), Mr. J.J. Bentley, Mr. Bertie Wills and Sir C. Powering.

THE MATCH

Around the ground were hundreds of players known in the world of football, while not the least interested of the spectators were the full complement of Tottenham Hotspur, who occupied specially reserved seats to the left of the Pavilion, and whose faces plainly denoted the fact that their one great ambition was to have another go for that small, but much valued trophy. Of course, the inevitable cinematograph was in evidence, one intrepid operator going so far as to almost hang on by his eyebrows to

---

27 Stived – [archaic] crowded.

the Stand roof, while others with cameras of all descriptions covered the ground and snapped groups when they thought fit. The Crystal Palace Band discoursed a pleasing selection of music, while on the opposite side of the turf, the occasional sound of one of those terrible instruments guaranteed by advertisement to "make your home happy," christened by an evident wit the melodion (smaller, much simplified version of an accordion), could be heard, but with these exceptions there was an absence of noise for a while, and the ever-increasing crowd simply awaited the coming of the men. As usual, the arrangements were perfection, and the writer never heard growl even from an indignant Pressman who might have applied too late for a seat at the long rows of wooden structures provided for their special use and the edification of the general public. At length the police cleared the ground in the easiest fashion, and the band having paid due respect "Our King," the crowd looked eagerly towards the Pavilion, and were soon rewarded by the arrival on the green sward of the Derby County eleven. The others were not long in following, and, clad in light blue shirts, formed a great contrast to the Peakites' deep red.

The sun was shining brightly when a start was made, but a breeze blowing from the cycle track end made the flags flutter, and it was a source of surprise to most after Derby had won the toss that they should prefer to play from the other. However, whether it was wise or not they did so, and a shout went up when Sagar set the ball in motion by just passing away to his inside left. The Lancastrians were at once the aggressors, and but for sturdy defence on the part of the County backs looked remarkably like scoring. With a strong half-back line, however, they were soon in neutral territory, and a moment later Fryer had to defend his citadel. Then one got an idea of the strength of the wind, for with plenty of force behind it the ball went into the air only to fall straight down to Mother Earth. To make matters worse clouds began to gather, and the one disadvantage at which Bury were placed was nullified. There was an absolute lack of that enthusiasm with which one is in the habit of associating the Cup Final, plainly showing who were favourites with the majority of the crowd, but at length a strong attempt at a cheer went up when Richards distinguished himself by making a very decent run. His kick at the termination was not good however, for in attempting to shoot he went wide of the mark. The County tried again, but with no better success, for the shrill whistle of Mr. Adams, the firm but impartial referee, told how Yorke was off-side just as he was sending the ball into the Bury net. A little deviation from ordinary footer was given by Morris, who treated the spectators to an acrobatic display all on his own, and one which made it pretty clear that he is quite conversant in the art of tumbling. Another was created when on one occasion the ball coming towards the sacred confines of the "Fourth Estate[28]," a bandsman peacefully reclining in front suddenly jumped and attempted to return it to the field. With two efforts he managed to effect his purpose, amidst the laughter of people, but he gave one the impression that the trombone was more in his particular line than the football. These were the only mirth-provoking incidents of the game, for there wasn't even the football dog to create a smile. There was no getting away from the fact that things were going flat, and when Bury continued to press hard, and twenty minutes had gone by, Ross scored a goal, the hearts of Derby County's supporters must have been affected. It was no fault of the Peakites' custodian that the ball went through, for the shot had to

---

28 The press [box] – an extension of the historical division of the Three Estates of the Realm: the clergy, the nobility, and the commoners.

pass several backs en route, and these were somewhat in the line of sight. A few minutes later a collision between Thorpe and Richards caused a cry to emanate from the lips of one of the players to "git oop," and townsmen smiled. One of the only genuine bursts of enthusiasm ensuing during the opening half, with the exception of that accompanying the opening goal, was when McEwen made a magnificent long dropping shot, which was equally cleverly fisted out of danger when it looked 1,000 to 1 on the ball going through. There was a great deal of off-side play on either side, but Bury were much the more sinned against than sinning. However, the half-time whistle sounded and the Lancashire players were ahead. That was all they cared about, and as they walked to their dressing-rooms a good reception awaited them.

Another was extended when they returned refreshed to the field. The Lancastrians were at once seen to advantage, but then Derby had the double misfortune of not only having a second point scored against them, but also of losing their already lamed goal-keeper. It came about through a collision with Sagar in front of goal, and both were injured so badly that the attendance of their trainers and an officer of the St. John's Ambulance Brigade (which, by the way, did excellent work, under the direction of the chief surgeon, Dr. Swayne) became requisite. Sagar recovered, but although Fryer was particularly plucky, it was no good, and he had to retire, while Morris was deputed to do his work in goal. From this point disaster followed disaster, and try how they would the County were unable to stave off defeat. Four more goals followed in quick succession, and when the whistle finally sounded Bury had established such a victory as has never been before recorded in connection with the Final of the Football Association Cup.

At the conclusion of the game the rival elevens were ushered into the enclosure, where that grand old man of football, Lord Kinnaird, awaited them, and, following on a fine speech, in the course of which he heartily congratulated the winners, presented the trophy to George Ross, the captain, and medals to either eleven. Ross very briefly replied, and then followed manly speeches from Mr. H.W. Lawson and Sir Thomas Rowe, after which the Cup was filled and passed round, whilst the winners were photographed with it in their midst. In the evening, while Bury were guests at a banquet given by Mr. H.W. Lawson at the Trocadero, Derby County were entertained at the Strand Theatre, where "The Chinese Honeymoon," under the able management of Mr. Byron Webber, jun., is nightly creating roars of laughter to crowded houses.

A DETAILED REPORT OF THE MATCH (from the same publication).

Ten minutes before the time due to begin hostilities a lusty shout announced the entrance of the Derbyshire men. As they trooped out from the pavilion end nearest the glassy pile, led by the veteran Archie Goodall, they looked a heavy-limbed crew, but probably the slack ruby jerseys above the dark blue pants lent the impression. A moment later a mighty shout from 10,000 Lancashire throats heralded the advent of George Ross and his men. As they tripped across the ring in their pale blue jerseys the Bury lads looked a sprightly, dashing lot, and a general survey gave the idea that they were a faster and gamer gang to deal with. As the favourites bolted about in their preliminary canters all around rose the murmurs of encouragement, more a deep sigh than articulate words. Half a dozen minutes before the time due to set the ball agoing on its momentous journey the rival captains advanced to spin the coin to the accompaniment of the warning words from friends around of "Good Old Garge" and "Haw, Archie." Thus early the teams were having it brought home to them that on the slopes of Sydenham Hill the lads from home were watching every move, on the ever varying chessboard with even greater intensity than probably the players themselves. The coin meant little or nothing for the brilliant sun of the early forenoon was somewhat obscured in a bank of clouds, and a general soft haze over the sky lent that fine steady light which players most desire, and in it's even distribution gives no advantage. The wind, too, was but a trifling factor. It piped to some tune, but came over the big stand, and the field of play lying under the lee of the structures, was but little disturbed by the elements. But whatever breath there was counted for nothing, blowing, as it did, across. But the almost proverbial fortune of the veteran skipper of the Rams did not desert him, and there was a rousing shout when it was noticed that he had guessed the coin. No more time was put to waste in idle play and amidst suppressed excitement the men lined up for the fray. Drawn in line, every man craning for the start, straining like a hound on the leash, they presented a sight for the athletic gods of Greece. And what a scene. The banked-up mounds with their tiers and tiers of eager faces. But the whistle has gone, so let us to the game and it's portents.

To Sagar fell the honour of giving the ball it's initial impetus, and amidst a pent-up yell the dapper little forward slipped the ball over to Wood. No signal could have been more effective for the united simultaneous action of 50,000 and more. The moment, to the absolute fraction of the second, Sagar gave the ball the light pass the sonorous volume rose, "Come on Darby, Daa-arby," or "Come on Bury, Bu-ury." But the men were slow at settling down. Wood, getting the ball in turn, passed it on to Richards, and in a nervous sort of way the outside man landed into touch. From the throw in there was an exchange of kicks between the halves, no progress being made by either side. In all big ties, where the issues are so great, it is always the way with the rival teams being a little unsettled to begin with. Bury got into their stride the quicker. Sagar leading the attack on Fryer. Methven cleared, and Goodall slipped the ball on to the left wing. The pair made little headway, however, McEwen bounding in on them and snipping the ball away to his forwards. To the delight of their supporters, the Bury forwards now settled down to something like their accustomed game. Sagar gave a long pass out, and Leeming and Plant, a beautiful combination, took the play right on Fryer. The outside man passed back, and Sagar let go a terrific drive which the Derby custodian did well to save. It was a great shot and a great save, and the efforts deserved the dual cheer. Some anxious moments were spent by the Derby supporters, but a mighty punt by Methven turned the venue, and Yorke intimated that he was in the mood by a shot which went past the post as if it had come out of a cannon's mouth. So near was the shave that from the higher parts of the hills the yell of "Goal! goal! goal!" went up. But it was not yet, Monteith placing the ball for a bye kick. From the goal kick Bury dashed down in ominous fashion, and a perfect hail of shots were rained on Fryer. Once Morris stepped in, and with a lovely clock kick sent the ball up field. The Derby right wing took up the pacing, and another rattler was sent bang at Monteith. It took him all his time to keep a hold of it and then throw clear before Boag was in on him. Play was thus early fast and fairly evenly distributed. The Bury forwards were the trickier, but in the play that had passed so far they were not so dangerous when they landed within shooting range. An exciting moment passed directly in front of Monteith. From a long, high kick by Archie Goodall they clustered round the Lancashire goal. The ball was headed out, and Davis went to it. He caught the ball on the wrong angle and sent it the wrong way, the ball going down the field instead of into the goal mouth. Archie Goodall's resource, however, came to the rescue, for, ever alert to such possibilities, he was lying ready, and catching the ball up banged it hard into the goal mouth. Now ensued the most exciting moments of the match so far. The Derby forwards clustered round and the Bury men packed their goal. Time after time the ball rose high, but never went out, and the struggle continued hard and fast, each and all of them taking and giving with a will the most solid of charges in a determination on the one hand to free the pressure and on the other to force the ball home. It was in such a moment, such a corner, that the player of the subtle powers of Steve Bloomer would have been worth a king's ransom, and many a sigh went up from a Midlander present for two minutes of the irresistible Steve. Not one of the Derby forwards could do it, and just when things were looking at the most crucial stage Thorpe was made out facing his own goal, and, taking a magnificent over-head kick, put the leather in territory far clear of any danger. It was a great struggle on both sides, and rather put heart into the Derby breast - for be it known that prior to the start the Bury men were pretty solid favourites. However they were not long to remain in this frame of mind, for the Bury men bore away in a body. Wood had the ball at his foot most of the way, and made a hard cross-shot. It reached Plant, and the latter sent in a hard, swift, low shot which Fryer did not quite get away. The ball went out as far as Leeming, but the forward failed to gather it, and the leather travelled on as far as George **Ross**. The Bury captain was in splendid position, and made a full force drive at the far corner of the goal, from where Fryer at the moment was standing. The Derby custodian had not had time to recover from the previous effort in stopping Plant's shot, and he stood no chance whatever stopping the ball, and so there it lay in the net. The first goal for Bury having been fittingly scored by the skipper of the team, Geordie Ross. It is needless to say that thunders of applause greeted the success, which was timed 20 min. from the start. The Derby men were in no way dismayed, and, answering the repeated calls of their well wishers, they went away from the centre in telling style. The attack was persistent, but the Lancashire defence was unshaken, and Lindsay and McEwen were always on the mark. Once a great yell rose, "Go on, Boag!" but Boag was charged off the ball, and Lindsay took the kick that might have been a goal. Away to the other end Sagar raced. The clever northern centre made the opposing backs travel at some pace, but in the end he was beaten off the ball. Only at the expense of a corner, however, which in its turn proved abortive. The Bury men were not to be shaken off easily, and just at the moment they looked like making some additions to their register. Methven, however, cleared, and in a rather haphazard style the Derby front rank made off, but they found, as before, the Bury backs as sound as a rock. McEwen especially was in remarkable form, and every time he made for the ball he got it. His kicking was beautiful and clean, and of great length. Just at this time it looked as if the Derby forwards were a beaten lot. The impression gained force as time after time they got opportunities from their halves, and as often McEwen or Lindsay stepped in and without almost apparent effort clipped the ball away. The two Bury backs seemed to have no trouble in doing this, and it was the too apparent ease with which they collared the ball every time that struck us that so far as Derby were concerned a goal would never come, whatever else Bury might accomplish. The Lancashire forwards were not doing much at this juncture, but they wakened up a bit soon. A fine combined run, in which Johnston, Sagar, and Plant were conspicuous, seemed likely, but when danger was most threatening Methven stepped in the breach and beat the opposition off. From the long kick of the Scotsman the Derby right wing got under weigh[29] but Boag when he had the ball passed to him made a poor show at shooting. A counter run by the Bury forwards was terminated by Richards sending wide. Some midfield play followed, and then a spasmodic rush by the Bury forwards resulted in a corner, which like all its predecessors, came to nothing. From the goal mouth scramble Boag, the Derby centre, who had been singularly ineffective, made away almost on his own. He darted down the field, and his great effort revived the drooping Derby hearts. The venue, which for some time had been all around Fryer, now turned completely to Monteith's end. The Derby forwards were fired with new life, and they went helter skelter to their work. Their passing was better, and their shooting had now more sting in it than at any time during the game. Monteith fisted out half a dozen shots, and the respective heads of McEwen and Lindsay got in the way of half a dozen more. It looked certain now that the Derby men would draw level, and from the surrounding slopes came any amount of lung power to buck them up. The Bury halves could do nothing to stem the rush, and McEwen and Lindsay were constantly in the thick of it. Some three minutes' had to run before the interval, and every effort was strained by Boag, Richards, and Davis. The latter especially was playing magnificently, and tricked Lindsay several times. A foul further brightened the Derby prospects, but the charge was cleared, and amidst the very hardest of pressure on Monteith the half time whistle went with the score:- Bury, one goal; Derby County, nothing.

During the interval the chances were pretty evenly regarded, the dash which the Derbyshire men had shown in the closing moments of the first moiety rather rehabilitating them in the good graces of their supporters. The restart, however, was almost remarkable, and somewhat upset the Derby theory. The Bury forwards pounced on the ball and dashed down. Sagar struck the crossbar with a tremendous shot, and then Leeming sent high over. Bury, in the opening seconds, monopolized proceedings. Such a terrific fusillade was kept up, such a regular stampede, as it were, on the Derby fortress that a goal at any moment looked like coming. The Derby men were simply off their feet, and could not follow the lightning passes of the Bury forwards. A lot of scrambling and dodging took place, and three minutes from the resumption the ball was banged into Derby's net for the second time. The play was at such a hurricane pace that it takes much longer to describe than the time it actually occupied. The Bury forwards had got into their stride, if you will accept the expression, like greased lightning. They were all over the Derby defence. The Bury men always had the ball, and it was more by chance than good guidance that Methven or Morris, or, the last obstacle, Fryer fell in the way of the sphere. What actually happened in getting the goal was this: Richards, who was making rings round Warren, took the ball down the line, and with a cross shot landed it in front of Sagar. The centre went in with the ball at his feet, and Fryer, with the intention of getting on centre before he had time to steady up and shoot, dashed out. The pair collided and fell to the ground in a heap, but instinctively, you might say, **Sagar** kicked the ball as he was bowled over. The two men lay on the ground, the big and the little 'un, and the offending ball rolled quite slowly into the corner of the net. Sagar had got right through the defence, and the Derby backs had no time to cover their goal. Sagar promptly recovered, but Fryer seemed in rather a bad plight, and had to be carried out of play. He lay on the ground for long

---

29   under weigh {archaic spelling} – moving off (from the nautical to weigh anchor). Now usually spelled 'under way.'

time, and eventually play was resumed without him, Morris going between the sticks. A man short Derby held no chance, but the first blush of excitement over, the Bury men quietened down a trifle. The Derby men had a bit of a look in, Methven taking a big risk the ring in going practically as a fourth half-back. The sturdy Scot was always well up the field, and for a little the game paid, the Midland forwards getting many chances. However, they made little use of them. The pace they showed in the last moments of the first half had died away like candle in a breeze, and anything they put up was readily repelled by McEwen and Lindsay. Monteith being very rarely called upon to handle. Several times the Bury forwards got away, but Methven's tactics of standing so well forward upset the calculations, and they generally found themselves under the ban of the offside rule. They tumbled at last to the plan of the canny Scot, and once they saw the ruse, disaster rapidly followed disaster to the cause of Derby. The turn came by Wood who engineered the ball himself. Tired by the repeated off-side whistle he took no risks, but on meeting Methven he kicked the ball hard ahead and went after it himself. It was a race between two men Wood and Methven, and from the goal Morris saw that there would only be one man in it, and as this was not Methven, Morris took the law of goalkeeping into his own hands, and bolted from under the sticks to meet the oncoming Wood. In daring style, Morris flung himself at the ball and stopped it, at the same time upsetting Wood, and lying prone the Derby custodian *pro tem*, could do nothing, and **Leeming** having followed up had an open goal presented to him. It was a stirring bit of play, told in a measure on the part of Morris, but the actual taking of the goal was a weak business. There can be no doubt Morris made an error in leaving his goal. If he had waited sleuth-like he might have seen Wood overrun himself, so hard a pace was he going at. Poor Fryer was lying watching all this and lame as he was he instantly up and stood ready for action. But it was no good, Bury had been fairly roused. From the centre, Thorpe jumped on, and took the pass from Boag to Richards. He dribbled in splendid fashion down alone, and was evidently very keen to score himself. He held tenaciously on to the ball, and finally had a parting shot. Fryer limped along the line, and just succeeded in pitching himself full length at the ball. He had managed to turn it to the left a little, but it was only a few yards, and **Wood** pressing up sent the ball back in. This was the fourth goal, and of course, the game was now lost and won. The time gone was just inside twenty minutes. From the centre Derby made no headway. The forwards had no pluck in them, and Richards, of the light blues, took possession, and rattled all on his own down the touchline. He overran the ball and Morris, who was again in his regular position, let his front line away. The five rallied to the old cause, but it was only for a moment or two. Monteith was called upon and cleared easily, and Boag followed with a long drive over the bar. From the goal kick-off the Lancashire men made away and although leading by so many goals spared no effort, and certainly spared not their opponents. The right wing attacked briefly, and Sagar finished with a pretty shot. Leeming tried unsuccessfully, and immediately afterwards **Plant** got possession, and sent the ball home for the fifth time. This was but three minutes after the fourth goal, and while it sent the Bury contingent into raptures took all interest out of the tie. Fryer, evidently suffering much pain, and seeing the hopelessness of his cause, left the field before the ball was kicked from the centre, and at the same time thousands of people moved away. With ten men the Derby lot made a feeble attack, but Monteith kicked up and mildly fisted away as if anxious to give the poor old Rams a chance. In a Trice the Bury forwards were on the other tack. **Leeming** dodged round Methven and found himself with only Morris to beat. This he did very easily, and with the sixth goal went up the record figures for the Cup final. It was all over now, and the closing stages were but a farce. The Bury forwards kept popping the ball from one head to the other, the County men having no heart to stop their dodging and tricking. Just at the end the Derby men got down, and hopes rose that they would blot out some of the calamity by putting on at least one goal, but they failed, and the whistle sounded with the Bury scroll unbroken.

RESULT: Bury 6 - Derby County 0

BURY: Monteith (goal); Lindsay and McEwen (backs); Johnston, Thorpe and Ross [1] (halves); Richards, Wood [1], Sagar [1], Leeming [2] and Plant [1] (forwards).
DERBY CO.: Fryer (goal); Methven and Morris (backs); Warren, Goodall and May (halves); Warrington, Yorke, Boag, Richards and Davis (forwards).
Referee: Mr. John Adams (Birmingham).

Manchester Evening News - Monday 20 April 1903
THE CUP VICTORS.
Bury Team Leave London - Enthusiastic Send-Off.

The Bury team left London at 10.15 this morning. It was a happy family party of twenty, but might have been swollen several times its number if the saloon which the Midland Railway Company had attached to its Birmingham train would have held all who desired to travel with the Association Cup, and the team which had so brilliantly won it. There was a crowd to witness the departure of the cup holders of 1903 which, if comparatively small in size, made up for its deficiency in that respect by its enthusiasm. The week-end had been spent in such a scene of excitement and pleasure-seeking that it seemed almost a positive relief to the team to be going in for work once more at West Bromwich, though nobody was prepared to say that much success was was to be expected in the encounter with West Bromwich. The team, with Messrs. Wardle, Duckworth and Unsworth, accompanied also by Mr. Hamer, left the Tavistock Hotel at 9.30 and reached St. Pancras a quarter of an hour before the train was due to leave. They had the cup with them and it was the object of much solicitude, not only on the part of the team, but also of the spectators. The blue and white favours of those who accompanied the team had evidently never seen the rough and tumble of a final at the Palace. They were rather fresh from the draper's shop, and must have been purchased in honour of the victory of the Lancashire team.

The Custody of the Cup.

"But," said Mr. Wardle when he got the trophy inside the saloon, "did you ever see anything like this?" and he pointed with disgust to the case which contained the cup. It was an oak box, or rather the remains of one, for the various pieces of which it is composed seemed to have too great a tendency to fall away and were greatly indebted to a double cord for the hold they had on each other and the goblet enclosed by them. Mr. Wardle continued, "they don't seem to know how to take care of a cup when they get it in Sheffield and London. When we had it in Bury last time we got the case put into excellent order and see how it returns to us. I suppose we shall have to get it repaired again. However, we have got it and I think we shall know how to keep it."

The Arrival To-night.

Mr. Duckworth and he proceeded to unpack the cup and place it on the table near one of the windows of the saloon, so that it might be seen by all who cared to witness it as the train left the station. Mr. Duckworth was very proud of his team, and informed our representative who witnessed the departure that after playing the match at West Bromwich the party would proceed to Bury, arriving at Victoria Station, at ten o'clock to-night. There the saloon and the van behind it will be detached and run on by special engine to Bury, which town is expected to be reached between half-past ten and eleven o'clock. What is in store for them was unknown to the officials in London. Bury is having a full holiday to-day, it being Sheriff's day, and what the team would have been delighted with most would have been to return during the hours of daylight, but the West Bromwich match prevented this and the night air will have to be braved by those who wish to see the home-coming of the cup to Bury. From the station the party will proceed to the Derby Hotel, where the remainder of the evening will be spent in rejoicings over the success of the team.

Bury's Unique Record.

Mr. Duckworth pointed out that Bury's record was a unique one in regard to cup finals. If Derby have been unlucky, Bury on the contrary have been particularly successful. When they won the cup for the first time three years ago it was the proud boast of the club that in every case where the final stage of a cup competition had been reached, the trophy had always been won[30]. Since then nothing had happened to break that record, and the win at the Palace merely served to emphasize it. Whether the team would be as successful in the Manchester cup and the Lancashire Cup for both of which trophies the final is fixed for next week, remains to be seen.

Condition of the team.

It is not a team in the pink of condition that is to face West Bromwich this afternoon. The Cup final, though the Lancashire team was able to take matters comparatively easy, took a lot out of the men. The ground was so hard that scarce a man but is complaining of blistered feet, and the natural hilarity over the win and the excitement attendant on it have not served to put the men into a fit condition for a stiff match today. Hence, though Ross said that they would do their best to win the match, none was willing to stake his reputation on a win. As the train steamed out of the station the crowd on the platform gave vent to a hearty cheers and cries of "well played, Bury!" and "play up, Bury!" The team acknowledged the send off with the waving of hats through the window and from the platform at the rear of the saloon.

An ovation at Birmingham.

The Bury team drove through the streets of Birmingham this afternoon on the way to the West Bromwich Albion ground amid general cheering. The English cup was effectively displayed.

---

30 True with regards the F.A. Cup and Lancashire Cup but not so the Manchester Cup in which Bury had twice been beaten finalists.

Manchester Courier - Tuesday 21 April 1903
BACK IN BURY - ENTHUSIASTIC WELCOME OF THE CUP WINNERS.

It may be true that prophets have no honour in their own country, but the saying does not apply to footballers. Leastways not in Bury. Ninety-nine people out of every hundred in that town prophesied that their pets would win the English Cup for the second time, on Saturday, and yesterday they laid themselves out to give a reception worthy of the occasion to the men who had not only justified their prophecy, but who had equalled the record of the famous Preston North End in 1889, when they went through the competition without having a goal scored against them and had also set up a new record in beating their opponents by six goals to none. True, there was another reason why Bury should throw off its work-a-day garb. For the third time in its history the town had been honoured by having the High Sheriff of the county chosen from the ranks of its citizens, and yesterday was the day fixed when he should commence his year of office. Hence the bulk of the mills were closed on Friday evening till this morning, and in the interval the town has worn a holiday aspect. The remarkable performance of the "Shakers" at the Crystal Palace on Saturday afternoon delighted, if it did not surprise, everybody in Bury, and every message received from the Metropolis regarding the doings of the victors was read and inwardly digested with the greatest avidity. The fact that Mr. Harry Lawson - the Unionist candidate in the recent bye-election, when Bury, according to many sensible folks, "went wrong" on the so-called corn tax - had entertained the team at the Trocadero after their splendid victory gave the liveliest satisfaction in the town, and the average working man of Bury is not likely to forget this thoughtful action when Mr. Lawson next visits "Simnel town." The streets were gaily decorated to honour Mr. Whitehead, the High Sheriff of the county - a fine representative sportsman - and he had just been heartily sent off by his townsfolk when the latter began to show their anxiety about the result of the League contest which was taking place at West Bromwich. A victory of three to one was enough to send even a Bury partisan home contented with himself and his favourites, and contented to wait with patience till the hour approached for the team to arrive, which was something about eleven o'clock. Five out of every six of the shops were closed and in darkness, and in consequence the streets were by no means brilliantly lighted by the arc-lamps that are few and far between, but the crowds of "younger Bury" that patrolled them were jolly to excess. Bolton-street and Rock-street, as well the offshoots, were thronged from eight o'clock onwards by two moving streams of people, all in best tempers, and most of them discussing football. The clatter of the Lancashire clogs were unheard; the twist of the Lancashire shawl was unseen. Everybody seemed in Sunday attire, and everybody seemed bent on enjoying themselves. Along the edge of the causeways street vendors, many of them the Manchester type, did roaring trade in mementoes of one kind and another, perhaps the most taking being a pictorial postcard which represented a member of the Derby County team receiving a Bury pudding which he could not swallow. Confetti was freely and indiscriminately distributed, and as soon ten o'clock turned the streams of people which had been passing to and fro in opposite directions as if by common consent turned towards the Bolton-street railway station. The approaches to the platform were well and carefully guarded by servants of the company, who evidently fully recognised the responsibility of their positions. Towards half-past ten the Borough Brass Band started from the Athenaeum, followed by upwards of a hundred members of that institution bearing lighted torches, and brakes were engaged to convey the victorious team on their triumphant procession through the town, whose people are so proud of them.

It was close upon eleven o'clock, however, when the special train from Manchester steamed into the station. Mr. Alfred Wardle, the chairman of directors; Mr. Albert Duckworth, the vice-chairman; and Mr. James Unsworth were in charge of the team and in charge of the cup as well, and along with the players they were received and heartily welcomed by the Mayor (Councillor Duxbury) and other leading townspeople. The Mayor warmly complimented George Ross, the captain, on the record achievement of himself and his men, and then, amidst deafening cheers of the assembled thousands, mingled with the strains of the bands, the procession moved off and paraded the chief streets of the town. All along the route the cheering was continuous, and when at last a halt was made in front of the Derby Hotel the players had the greatest difficulty in saving themselves from their friends. Thanks chiefly to Mr. A.E. Dearden, the youngest member of the board of directors, who had left London in order to fix up the programme in Bury, the arrangements worked out admirably, and, no doubt, not the least pleasing to the tired if delighted players was a midnight repast in the "Derby."

A tongue-in-cheek account of the great day:

Sporting Life - Monday 20th April, 1903
BY OUR HUMOUR SEEKING REPORTER)

"This right for the Crystal Palace, mater?"
"Yes a through train old man."
"Well, thank goodness" said the presumed leader of the little party, as they bundled into the train at Ludgate Circus, and then turning to a companion said, rather sorrowfully, "You see Ike, I was right after all." That gentleman did not respond, but looked the other way, and it was not until the Elephant and Castle was reached and passed that the tale of their woes were unfolded. A merry little party of seven had travelled up from a remote place in Leicestershire. They made up their minds to see the final under any circumstances, and literally did not care a jot which clubs were playing - it was the final and that was enough. Only one of the party, "Ike," had been up to London before, and consequently he took command for the time being and volunteered to take his companions down to the Mecca of socker football. Again the adage was proved to the hilt, "that a little knowledge is a dangerous thing," for proceeding down the Euston-road, King's Cross Station struck the view of the leader, and also the words Alexandra Palace. Not bothering any further, they took train for Wood Green, determined to be in good time and secure a good pitch. Of course, when they arrived there it was only to find out that a race meeting was on hand. This led to an emergency meeting being called there and then. Ike proposed that they stayed to see the races, but failed to get a seconder, the opinion of the other six being that, having set out to see the final, they were going so to do under any circumstances, and so, returning to town, they became my travelling companions, and a jollier lot of fellows, with but one exception - and even he thawed before our arrival at the Palace - no one could wish to meet. Whether they took me for a walking encyclopedia bound in "calf" cannot be said. At any rate I had to answer a thousand and one questions, and when the express at length reached its

destination, after accomplishing the journey at the rate of about a mile every six minutes, they were enthusiastic over the chances of the rivals, but pinned their faith to the County, not that they knew anything about their form or troubled in the least what Bury had done or could do. If they had come from Yorkshire they would have gone nap upon the Lancastrians, but Derby being nearer to them than the County Palatine was all sufficient for their choice. That their hopes were blighted did not seem to affect them to any appreciable degree, as when I came across them later on, Bury then being four up, they enthusiastically declared they had never seen a better match in their lives. Evidently they had seen but few. Outside the Palace were dozens of "char-a-bangs," which had deposited their loads of passengers, who had taken advantage of the glorious Springlike weather to travel by road. Bicyclists were there in strong evidence, very strong, more especially when the poor belated pedestrian wished to cross the road, and remembered that he had forgotten to renew his policy with the Accidental Company; there is, however, one redeeming trait in the character of the Saturday afternoon cyclist, if you stand still, he will ride up the one side of you, and down the other, simply remarking, "A bit of rough road that;" and when you are still in doubt as to whether an earthquake has come along, or your mother-in-law has made a flank attack upon you with her umbrella, coolly looks around, and rings his bell, probably to let you know that it is safe, and he has no intention of proceeding against you for any damage to his machine, which, to say the least of it, is remarkably consoling, if you can only look at in that light. For the past twenty years business and pleasure have taken me to the venue of the Cup final, but never to one like that of Saturday last; there was not a "favour" to seen outside the Palace. Those good old-fashioned cards, which used to be sported in the hats advising the rivals to up, had evidently had their day and fallen into disrepute, and, to all intents and purposes, the visitors to the great game were upon a pilgrimage rather than a holiday outing. Not a mouth organ was to be heard, or a concertina to be seen, and even those generally loquacious gentry, the knights of the whip, were comparatively silent, retaining their fund of wit and humour for some other occasion. Finding that there was but little to be gained by mingling with the crowd outside, I naturally wended my way towards the scene of action, trusting that a little more life might be infused, and fortunately such was the case, for on teaching the terrace a couple of youngsters were busily engaged settling a dispute over some trivial affair or another, and were hard at work, endeavouring to improve each other's features. Well, even this was better than nothing at all, and personally I was somewhat sorry when an old Birmingham friend separated the champions for fistic honours, and advised them never to fight again without there was something hanging to it. Inquiring how many had come up from the Hardware village the reply was only about five hundred. You see there was no local interest in the match or otherwise there would have been more people here than there are. Fancy what the gate would have been if Aston Villa and Millwall had been left in. At least thirty thousand would have come up from Brum alone. Just at this moment the welcome strains of harmony were heard, and approaching the joyful party who were basking in the sun, the footballers lament was heard. The two verses I caught were as follows:

I'll never play at football any more,
I'm black and blue and very sore.
They broke my collar bone
   and then they took me home.

I'll never play at football any more.

I'll never play at football any more,
They knocked out my teeth and broke my jaw.
To them, perhaps, it was fun
   to see me look so glum.
I'll never play at football any more.

There was every appearance that some of them would have no chance at any rate for some considerable time for a venturesome climber had gained a point of vantage, but had evidently overlooked the fact that branches of trees are not built of cast iron, and consequently will only support a certain weight. An ominous crack and down sailed the branch upon which he had ensconced himself. How on earth he managed to escape must remain a mystery. He did so, and that sufficed in a dual respect - he was safe, and I was warned off the climbing. It had been my intention to join the birds in the branches, but wiser council prevailed. I remember the lecture and the accompanying castigation of years ago, when, against strict orders. I went birds-nesting; and when I say that my dear old pedagogue could have given Solomon a stone and a beating over any course where sparing the rod and spoiling the child was concerned, it will be readily understood that at least one reminiscence remains of the bygone I days, and as I sorrowfully glanced towards the sky I distinctly remembered his final words, "If you would only try to climb the tree of knowledge instead of going birdsnesting you might leave the hangman to break your neck in due time." Notices in profusion were posted around the ground pointing out the danger of climbing the trees - simply a waste of printers' ink. No one who rushed to get skywards, and were able to do so, paid the slightest attention; and these were not the only coigns of vantage taken advantage of, for, wherever you would look around the playing pitch improvised stands were in evidence, and, though there was a great falling off in the attendance, full advantage was taken of the slopes, and thousands had taken up their positions long before the game was started. With a roar that reminded one of Derby Day, the cry went up, "They are off!" and those outside the enclosures and stands knew that the struggle for the Cup had commenced. Passing along in search of whatever humour was to be found, and be it said there was very little, I approached one of Messrs. Lyon's temporary establishments, and was accosted thusly: Jack (one of the names given to me by sponsors), "come here and decide a Question." The speaker was one who had figured in several final ties, and can boast of at least three gold medals. With him were many old football players, some of whom I knew, and the others was duly introduced to. "Well," I asked, "What is the matter in discussion?" and was somewhat surprised when asked "If they had come to the Palace to drink beer or see the game?" I gave an evasive reply, and was then told that amongst them they possessed two briefs for the ring, could not get any more, and so were determined to stick together, which I presume they did at any rate. After vainly trying to persuade a policeman to run me in for some imaginary offence or another, I condescended to leave the then abode of bliss and meander towards the slopes. The dealers in colours and favours were shouting themselves hoarse, and then failed to do any trade, whilst the itinerant musicians, who were duly armed with banjos and mandolins, looked on with sorrowful eyes, no one wanted music, and but a few raised a cheer when Bury put on their first goal. Proceedings became a shade more lively after half time, and when the representatives of the Red Rose scored a couple of goals in quick succession, it was astonishing to see the sudden display of blue and white favours. Where had they sprung from? A thick and fast supporter of the Peakites declared that they would never have been sported if his little lot had been winning, and then, is strict confidence of course, showed the red and white favour pinned inside his coat. This explained the apparent mystery. By this time what little interest there was in the match had evaporated, and the sound of the referee's whistle for time came as a boon and a blessing. For once in a way there were very few ladies present, probably they dreaded the chill of the evening. Upon enquiry at the St. John's Ambulance tent, Dr. F.G. Swayne, the surgeon in charge, and whom I recognised as an old Cantab and ex-member of the Richmond and Blackheath F.C., said that there were but few trivial accidents to be recorded. There seemed to be but one opinion amongst the spectators when wending their way towards the railway stations, and that was they could not imagine how Derby County got into the final. The trains were soon packed. Not so the other vehicles, for those who had gone by road preferred to return by rail.

A Bury effort goes wide of the post

F.A. Cup Winners - 1903

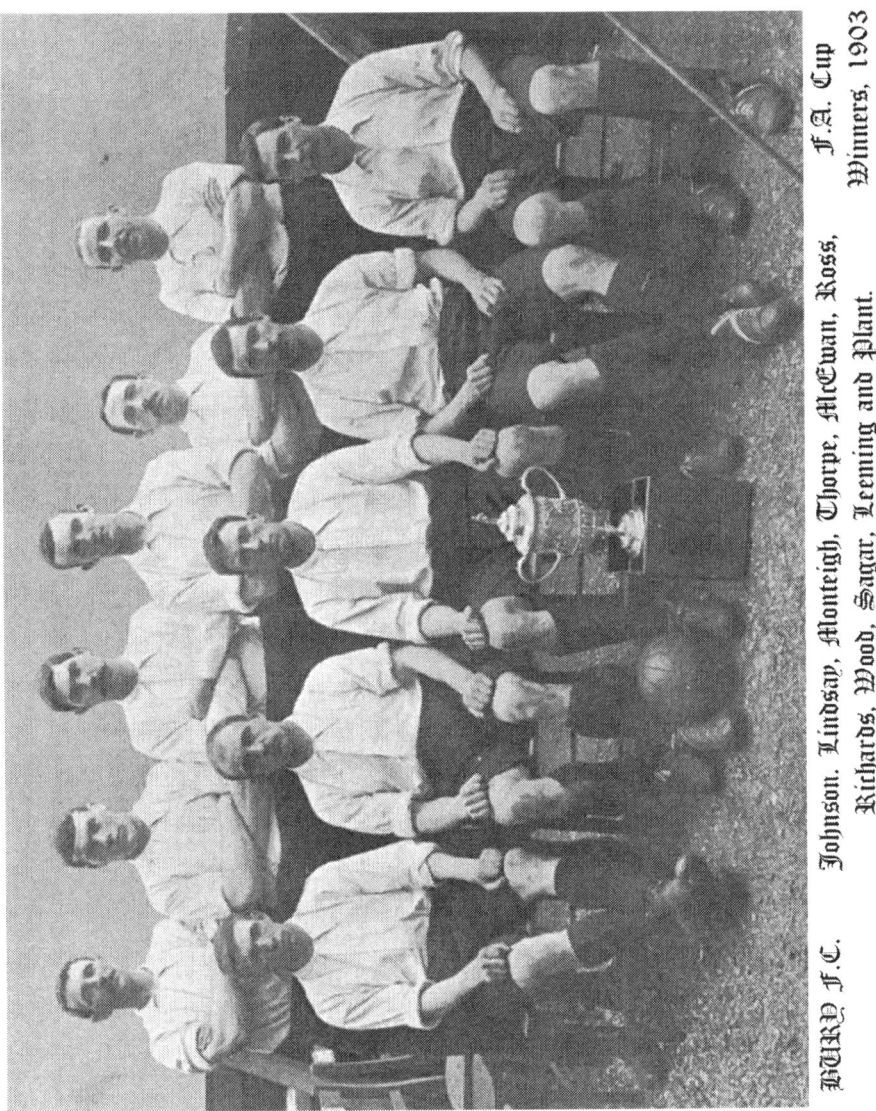

BURY F.C.   Johnson, Lindsay, Monteith, Thorpe, McEwan, Ross,   F.A. Cup
Richards, Wood, Sagar, Leeming and Plant.   Winners, 1903

The Final Tie for the Football Association Cup
Derby County and Bury at the Crystal Palace.

DRAWN BY ERNEST PRATER

The final tie in the annual competition for the Football Association Cup was played on Saturday at the Crystal Palace in the presence of over 63,000 spectators. Bury and Derby County were the competitors, and the Lancashire team, who during all the preliminary games had not lost a goal, won easily by 6 goals to nothing. The sketches illustrate the following incidents:—

No. 1—Attending to the injured goalkeeper
No. 3—Bury scoring
No. 2—Wearing the colours and carrying umbrellas of rival teams
No. 4—Travellers from the north who slept through the match

What Happened Next

Bury were only the third club in the history of the competition (after Clapham Rovers in 1880 and Preston North End in 1889 [Not counting The Wanderers in 1973 who received a bye to the final]) to win the trophy without conceding a single goal at any stage of the competition. Bury possess the unique record of doubling their score to date in the competition at both the Semi-Final and Final stages, whilst their six goal tally in the Final remains a record for that stage of the competition. The victory also maintained their remarkable record of success in Cup Finals, as did adding both the Lancashire Cup and the Manchester Cup (shared) to their tally again that season.

Manchester Courier - Tuesday 28 April 1903
LANCASHIRE CUP FINAL

Bury are enjoying football as keenly as they did in September last, and there were 8,000 spectators around the Gigg-lane enclosure last night, when Everton were met in the final tie of the Lancashire Cup competition. Bury were without Monteith and Sagar, Montgomery and Lamberton coming into the team. Settle and Creely were absentees from the Everton side.

Everton exhibited pretty work at the outset, twice getting dangerously near the goal. When Bury got going they were more effective and after the right wing had beaten Balmer, his colleague, Henderson, chipped in and saved what seemed a certain goal. There were numerous exciting incidents in the Everton goal, but the backs defended capitally, and when they were beaten Whitley proved a capital custodian. Bury could not penetrate the defence, and in the last minute of the first half their own goal had a narrow escape, one of the forwards shooting wide when the goal was unprotected. At half-time there was no score.

After the interval the game was full of interest. Both sets of forwards worked capitally, and but for the excellent defence goals must have accrued. At length Bury's effective work produced the opening goal, **Leeming** shooting through after good work by Richards. This was after fifteen minutes' play, and to the end the match was brimful of exciting incidents. Whitley was repeatedly saving, but now and again got away, and the result was not a certainty until the finish.

Mr. Woolfall, the President of the Lancashire Association, handed the cup to Bury.

Result: Bury 1 - Everton 0

Full teams not available but appear from the commentary to have been largely representative on both sides.

Manchester Courier - Thursday 30 April 1903
MANCHESTER CUP FINAL AT CLAYTON, UNUSUAL ISSUE.

Played on the Manchester United ground last evening, before 15,000 spectators. **Plant**, from a header by Leeming, scored a splendid goal for Bury after fifteen minutes. From a penalty **Meredith** scored for City. Early in the second half **Threlfall**, from a scramble in front of goal, added the second for City, whilst Monteith was on his back. **Lamberton**, however, equalised. Owing to bad light extra time could not be played. It was arranged that the clubs remain joint holders until September, when the match may be replayed. There were fully 15,000 people at Clayton last evening, the gate receipts amounting to £414. Bury did not quite effect their purpose of finishing the season possessing themselves of three cups, but still they had the satisfaction of retaining an unbeaten record in such competitions, their draw against Manchester City being a very creditable one. With to-day being the last day of the football season, there was scarcely time to have the tie replayed, and the Manchester Association decided that the clubs concerned should be joint holders of the trophy until next September, when the tie may be replayed. Medals of equal merit are to be awarded to the players of both sides, a procedure which is accounted most satisfactory.

Regarding the play, it was on the whole fairly even. It was a beautiful effort, after a quarter of an hour's play, that led to the English Cup holders' first goal. The ball came to Richards, who headed to Wood, while the latter fed Plant, who, fully twenty yards from goal, applied his left foot to the object and into the far corner of the net it flew. Subsequently Richards handled just within the penalty line. The affair seemed somewhat accidental, but the referee awarded a penalty, and Meredith, with Monteith coming out of goal, scooped the ball over the custodian's head and into the net it went.

Eight minutes after change of ends Threlfall gave the City the lead, the clever left wing forward finding the net in consequence of Monteith slipping down. Though a goal behind, Bury never lost hope. Thorpe and Johnston working effectively in the half-back line and giving the quintette in front of them plenty of openings. Wood, who had filled the centre forward position with little success, was ordered to partner Richards after the City had got in front, Lamberton going centre. This change immediately proved fruitful. Lamberton from a corner heading through and making the scores level.

On the whole Bury had a slight pull on the game, but they badly missed the services of Sagar, Wood in the position previously alluded to being much his inferior. Thorpe was the pick of the Bury halves, although Johnston and Ross were very effective, the last-named preventing Meredith from getting away though kicking into touch. The defence of both sides were pretty safe. Regarding the City front line Threlfall and Meredith were the shining stars, the last-named putting in several centres which deserved a better fate. As half-back Frost and McOustra, as usual, were in evidence.

Result: Manchester City 2 - Bury 2

Full teams not available but appear from the commentary to have been largely representative on both sides.

In fact, the final tie was not replayed that season and the two clubs shared the honour. Remarkably, the same two sides contested the Final again the following season with a similar result, the game again resulting in a draw. On this occasion a replay was staged the following December when Bury run out 4-0 winners.

At the end of the 1902/03 season Bury's annual statement of accounts showed a profit on the season of £1455. From this charitable donations were made of 50 guineas to Bury Infirmary and £20 to the Mayor's Distress Fund (to help those affected by the depression in the cotton trade).

All of the League players signed on again for the following with the exception of James McEwen, who returned to one of his former clubs, Luton Town, and was replaced at right-back by the signing-on of his near namesake, Robert McEwan

Bury finished their League campaign in eighth place. Two years later they finished second from bottom but escaped relegation due to the First Division being extended that season, and afterwards maintained their place among the elite until 1912.

The End

If you enjoyed this book, please watch out for other titles in the Season Scrapbook series.

Printed in Great Britain
by Amazon